THE WORKS OF SHAKESPEARE

EDITED FOR THE SYNDICS OF THE
CAMBRIDGE UNIVERSITY PRESS
BY
SIR ARTHUR QUILLER-COUCH
AND   JOHN DOVER WILSON

THE MERCHANT OF VENICE

THE MERCHANT
OF VENICE

CAMBRIDGE UNIVERSITY PRESS

Published by the Syndics of the Cambridge University Press
Bentley House, 200 Euston Road, London, NW1 2DB
American Branch: 32 East 57th Street, New York, N.Y.10022

ISBNS:
0 521 07545 9 hard covers
0 521 09488 7 paperback

First published 1926
*Reprinted 1953 1962
First paperback edition 1968
Reprinted 1969 1973

*Places where editorial changes or additions intro-
duce variants from the first edition are, when possible, marked by a date [1952, 1962] in square brackets.

First printed in Great Britain at the University Press, Cambridge
Reprinted in Great Britain by Hazell Watson & Viney Ltd,
Aylesbury, Bucks

CONTENTS

THE MERCHANT OF VENICE

I

For the text of this play we have pretty plain sailing; being left with three not very dissimilar versions amid which to steer, and now enabled by labour and ingenuity of previous students to arrange them strictly in order of merit. They are two Quartos and the 1623 First Folio. The whole question of the provenance of the text, as we have it, will be found very fully discussed in a subsequent *Note on the Copy*: but the conclusion comes very simply to this. There were two Quartos, both dated 1600, from either of which the 1623 Folio might have derived its authority: but one of these, and the one long taken as the better and called the 'First Quarto,' is now ascertained to have been fraudulently ante-dated on the title-page by Jaggard, who issued it as one of a series in 1619. So we come back for primary reliance on what is generally known as the 'Second' or 'Heyes' Quarto, the title of which is reproduced in facsimile on p. 1.

II

With the 'sources' of *The Merchant of Venice* we have (historically) even less reason to worry ourselves. The play includes three plots derived from old story and interwoven or adjusted by Shakespeare as best he could contrive. But these three plots—or two and a half of them—are to be found in *Il Pecorone* (or 'The Gaby'), a book of tales by one Ser Giovanni, supposed to have been compiled in 1378 but not published until 1558[1].

[1] An English translation by W. G. Waters was published in 1897, doubtless at the instance of the late A. H. Bullen. (London: Lawrence & Bullen.)

Who this 'Ser Giovanni' was admits anyone who enjoys the licence of conjecture to any width of it. But no one who reads the following brief summary of the First Tale of the Fourth Day (it is worked on the Boccaccio-Straparola pattern) will need to seek further for the source of the *Merchant of Venice* save in excess of that pedantry which is but idleness of the mind. Put in brief, the story comes to this:

A youth of Venice, Giannetto, is financed by his godfather Ansaldo on three voyages supposedly to trade at Alexandria, but coasting off a mysterious port of Belmonte he learns from the master of his ship of a lady whose person and riches are to be won at a great peril and determines to try his fortune. The terms of the wooing are curious: he has to remain awake through the night, or he loses the lady and forfeits his cargo. He fails twice: but on the third voyage he succeeds through the warning of a waiting-woman that his wine has been drugged. He avoids the drug and wins the lady. But the trouble is that for this last voyage his godfather has only been able to furnish him by borrowing ten thousand ducats from a Jew, on the unholy contract that if the bond be not met by St John's Day, the creditor shall have, from whatever part of the body he chooses, one pound of Ansaldo's flesh.

In the wedding and the festivities that follow, the ingrate Giannetto forgets his godfather's deadly peril; until one evening, on the balcony with his bride, he watches a troop of craftsmen go by bearing torches and on a casual enquiry is told that they are marching to pay their vows at St John's Church on the festival of the Saint. Thereupon he remembers the forfeit and the peril, and is struck with an anguish of remorse.

His wife, extracting the story from him, gives him a hundred thousand ducats and bids him ride post to save his godfather at whatever cost; Giannetto does so: but arrives at Venice in a sweat only to find that Ansaldo, though on the hope of bidding him farewell briefly respited, is under the law of Venice a doomed man.

The Jew, who has conceded this remand, will have no further mercy. Not for a hundred thousand ducats nor for all the money that rich Venice can raise will he forgo his claim to carve the flesh of this Christian. He holds his bond, and the law of Venice is righteously strict.

Better wits are at work. Prompt upon Giannetto and his vain intercession there arrives at an inn in the city a young Doctor of Laws of Bologna, who is of course —let us call her by Shakespeare's name—Portia in disguise. The host informs her of this desperate affair which is the talk of the city. She commands these good Venetians not to be afraid; by some process has prosecutor and defendant haled into presence, and works the Jew's confusion much as it is worked in our play.

Then, much as in our play, the grateful Giannetto visits her with the proffer of a hundred thousand ducats for her conduct of the case. Portia will take no fee at all save—on an afterthought—'that ring on your finger.' Giannetto is loth to part with it, but in the end does so. Thereupon follows the *éclaircissement* we expect. 'Sir, husband, where is my ring? You have given it to some other woman, to some sweetheart of Venice.' 'I have given it to no woman but to a grave young Doctor of Law.' 'I say you had better have abode in Venice to take your pleasure with your wantons. I hear they all wept when you left them.'

Giannetto burst into tears and, greatly troubled, cried, 'You swear to what cannot be true': whereupon the lady, perceiving from his tears that she had struck a knife into his heart, quickly ran to him and embraced him, laughing heartily the while she showed him the ring and told him everything[1].

[1] The story has been epitomised at greater length and in his own great manner by Dr Johnson, to whose edition we refer the reader.

From this epitome the reader can draw no other conviction but that Shakespeare or (to speak cautiously) some earlier playwright on whose work Shakespeare improved, took two of the three inwoven plots of the *Merchant of Venice*, (*a*) the pound-of-flesh business, and (*c*) the ring imbroglio, straight out of this selfsame tale in *Il Pecorone*. As for the intermediate (*b*) or casket-plot, a brief reflection will convince him that this too —the lover's testing—is implicit in the same original, though, clearly for dramatic purposes, it had to be altered. The original here is in fact at least as old as the story of Odysseus and Circe. A mariner enters a strange port. The Lady of the Land, a witch, espies his anchoring from her palace windows of *Belmonte*—περισκέπτῳ ἐνὶ χώρῳ, a place of wide prospect. The usual or typical story tells of an adventurer from the sea who is entertained and taken to bed by the enchantress, on the terms that if he fell asleep in the night, he is turned into a swine or some other beast or forfeits his manhood or, at any rate, his cargo, and to ensure his default he is given a night-draught of drugged wine. But clearly this story of

> magic casements, opening on the foam
> Of perilous seas, in faëry lands forlorn

cannot be presented dramatically. And so our playwright, whoever he was, cast back to medieval legend for another old lover's test, which he could easily borrow from the *Gesta Romanorum*, or indeed from anywhere —the test of the three Caskets. More shall be said presently upon this ages-old tradition of the suitor's choice which, usually a matter of triads, haunts mythology and fairy-tale wherever we explore them; as does the luck of the youngest of three brothers, and the enchantress and the Laidly Worm who is transformed into a lovely bride by a kiss. The reader will have noted that in the story of the Lady of Belmonte in *Il Pecorone* she is, as

though it were taken for granted, thus transformed.
From a witch she turns, at touch of lip, to a devoted and
capable wife.

III

So here one has three motives which mingle well
enough in a medieval tale but do not consort at all as
themes for a drama. We need raise here no question of
a Shakespeare who wrote from another man's work, or
revised or re-revised it. Inquisition by Shakespearian
scholars on the lines to-day being followed will assuredly
lead, or help to lead, to a clearer text. But the plays
remain, for truly critical purposes, as we have them: and
anyone who, with a tolerable ear, has listened to Shakespeare's music all his life, may be excused for example
for doubting if more confident men be really able to sift
out Shakespeare from Fletcher in *Henry VIII* or *The
Two Noble Kinsmen*—and still, all debts acknowledged,
one must affirm that the Shakespeare a reader or a man
in the theatre enjoys, and the only one on whom a critic
can employ his skill to help towards judgment and enjoy-
ment, is the Shakespeare we have and not any guessed
partitions of him. To put this particularly of the *Merchant of Venice*, everyone knows that Stephen Gosson
writing in 1579 in his *Schoole of Abuse* and referring to
some plays above any moral reproach, mentions one
called by him *The Iew*, 'showne at the Bull' and
'representing the greedinesse of worldly chusers and
bloody minds of Usurers'; and that a deal of speculation
has been spent upon Shakespeare's indebtedness to this
old play; and Gosson's description of it may be taken,
even probably, to cover the casket-scenes and Shylock's
bond in some 'original' derived from *Il Pecorone*. But
what can that speculation, however likely, amount to
for any purpose but to employ idleness? We have the
Il Pecorone tale; and *The Merchant of Venice* in which
Shakespeare made a drama of it, leaving to us, whatever

reservations we make, a mightily effective play. It is
also for those curious about his genius, a strangely in-
triguing play: for Shakespeare, more than any dramatist,
could defeat definition among tragedy, comedy and
romance. Years after this experiment he invited us to
laugh at Polonius pulling his beard and solemnly dif-
ferentiating 'tragedy, comedy, history, pastoral, pastoral-
comical, historical-pastoral, tragical-historical, tragical-
comical-historical-pastoral, scene individable, or poem
unlimited.' We are dealing with a dramatist who more
than any other has overridden all these categories with
a negligent smile, and that (be it remembered) through
and after encounters at 'The Mermaid' with Ben
Jonson, hectoring layer down of the law as derived from
Aristotle and transmitted in practice through Seneca and
Plautus[1]. We may therefore in dealing with *The Merchant of Venice*, as in dealing later with *Antony and
Cleopatra*—in both of which plays we know, as accu-
rately as may be, his sources—ask how he did it.

IV

He did it almost always, if one may use the term, with
an instinctive economy. Chaucer has something of this
gift in handling his 'originals,' but Shakespeare has it in
a superlative degree. No one reading the *Life of Antony*
in North's *Plutarch* alongside of *Antony and Cleopatra*
can miss to marvel at the frugality of the converting
touch. So we take it, understanding (as we have surely
a right to do) that this overworked, constitutionally
indolent man, apparently careless of his dramatic work,

---

[1] Cf. Meres, 'As Plautus and Seneca are accounted the
best for Comedy and Tragedy among the Latines; so
Shakespeare among the English is the most excellent in
both kinds for the stage' (followed by a reference to *The
Merchant*) with Polonius' apostrophe 'Seneca cannot be
too heavy nor Plautus too light.'

once done, just operated upon the story as genius suggested throughout.

Now the first, or Shylock-Antonio story, is evident Tragedy. The Merchant corresponds at every point to the Aristotelian demand upon a tragic hero. He is a good man who, not by vice, but through some error, comes to calamity. So, up to a point—a definite point—Shakespeare conducts his drama up towards pure tragedy. He opens upon Antonio's gloom and foreboding of some heavy fate, obviously meant to be communicated at once to the audience—

> In sooth I know not why I am so sad,
> It wearies me, you say it wearies you;
> But how I caught it, found it, or came by it,
> What stuff 'tis made of, whereof it is born,
> I am to learn

—this upon a broken line and a pause through which we follow his moving. And this actual business of tragedy persists, through revel and carnival and masquers, noise of hautboys, choosing of caskets—to music and the music of a right woman's voice confessing and surrendering to love, straight to the point where Portia asks

Why doth the Jew pause?

If the Jew had not just been held at pause by that mastering question, if his hatred and revenge, racial and personal, had carried him an inch over that question, if, so to say, this very grand Hebrew had divorced his ducats from his daughter and cried out, 'Revenge I will have: afterwards tear me limb from limb,' under the law of Venice Portia's quibble had gone by the board, and the play must necessarily, from that instant, have reverted to the tragic conclusion its opening lines portend.

V

We must now consider Shylock: but we cannot consider him individually until we have laid our account with the attitude of our ancestors in Elizabeth's time towards the Jew in general, because that attitude differed so greatly from our modern tolerance. Legally, he was excluded from our country; and there is nothing like unacquaintance to foster hatred in general. The race has always, from Jacob's time, prospered on usury; and the Church backed, if it did not incite, the law, by its official execration of that practice as a sin against nature[1]. To be sure, a nation, prosperous as England was during the fifteenth and sixteenth centuries, exporting its wool to all known foreign markets and holding the most of the world's carrying trade on long voyages at sea, could not, and in fact did not, dispense with systems of credit and exchange. And even earlier, in the fourteenth century, we find a learned professor, Benvenuto da Imola, declaring—'he who practiseth usury goeth to hell, and he who practiseth it not tendeth to destitution.' Nevertheless, the enterprising English Merchant adventured under Canon Law, and after the way of men would relieve his conscience by putting his sin on a scapegoat. What scapegoat so obvious as the Jew, who notoriously bred money from money in Lombardy and elsewhere, and was a descendant of the murderers of Christ?

If we would put ourselves in the mind of the average spectator of the first performance of *The Merchant of Venice*, we can perhaps hardly fetch better illumination for ourselves than from the following passage of Thomas Coryate (1577?–1617), recounting how he, a visitor to Venice, found it neither improper nor impertinent to accost a Rabbi in the street, and suddenly to invite him to change his religion.

For when as walking in the Court of the *Ghetto*, I casually met with a certain learned Jewish Rabbin that spake good Latin, I insinuated myself after some few terms of com-

---

[1] See Dante, *Inferno*, XI, where the inhabitants of Cahors, notorious usurers, share the same circle with the men of Sodom.

pliment into conference with him, and asked him his opinion of *Christ*, and why he did not receive him for his Messias; he made me the same answer that the *Turk* did at *Lyons*, of whom I have before spoken, that *Christ* forsooth was a great Prophet, and in that respect as highly to be esteemed as any Prophet amongst the *Jews* that ever lived before him; but derogated altogether from his divinity, (and would not acknowledge him for the *Messias* and Saviour of the world, because he came so contemptibly, and not with that pomp and majesty that beseemed the redeemer of mankind.) I replied that we *Christians* do, and will even to the effusion of our vital blood confess him to be the true and only *Messias* of the world, (seeing he confirmed his Doctrine while he was here on earth, with such an innumerable multitude of divine miracles, which did most infallibly testify his divinity.) Withal I added that the predictions and sacred oracles both of *Moses*, and all the holy Prophets of God, aimed altogether at *Christ* as their only mark, in regard he was the full consummation of the law and the Prophets, and I urged a place of *Esay* unto him concerning the name *Emanuel*, and a virgin conceiving and bearing of a son; and at last descended to the persuasion of him to abandon and renounce his Jewish religion and to undertake the Christian faith, without the which he should be eternally damned. He again replied that we Christians do misinterpret the Prophets, and very perversely wrest them to our own sense, and for his own part he had confidently resolved to live and die in his Jewish faith, hoping to be saved by the observations of *Moses'* Law. In the end he seemed to be somewhat exasperated against me, because I sharply taxed their superstitious ceremonies. For many of them are such refractory people that they cannot endure to hear any terms of reconciliation to the Church of Christ.

If we consider the above, it will not astonish us that Antonio, a Christian gentleman, found it not incompatible with ordinary good manners to spit at a Jew on the Rialto.

Nay more, the Church held it right to proselytise Jews and bring them to the Christian fold even by force. The reader will doubtless recall Browning's *Holy-Cross Day*, written around the historical fact that the Jews in Rome were forced to attend an annual Christian sermon down to the nineteenth century; and this fact will cast a light back upon the alternative penalties pronounced by the Courts in Marlowe's *Jew of Malta*, and in the *Merchant of Venice*.

In Marlowe's play the State of Malta levies its tribute to the Turks by mulcting the Jews on the following conditions: (*a*) every Jew must hand over one-half of his estate, or (*b*) straightway become a Christian; or (*c*) if he refused either of these terms, his whole estate must be forfeited. Let this be compared with the penalties imposed on Shylock in Act 4 of our play.

We have said enough to indicate the general attitude of Christians towards Jewry, though perhaps this enmity is better indicated in its grudging and gradual relaxation as Browning suggests this in his *Filippo Baldinucci on the Privilege of Burial*—dated by him 1676, a hundred years or so later than *The Merchant*:

> 'No, boy, we must not'—so began
> My Uncle (he's with God long since)
> A-petting me, the good old man!
> 'We must not'—and he seemed to wince,
> And lost that laugh whereto had grown
> His chuckle at my piece of news,
> How cleverly I aimed my stone—
> 'I fear we must not pelt the Jews!'

This above all should not be forgotten, that the Plantagenets who all along protected, by special enactments, their financiers, the Jews, were compelled by popular hatred to banish them from the realm, never to return until re-admitted under Oliver Cromwell. But there seems in 1594 to have been a particular recrudescence of this general hatred over one Roderigo Lopez, a Portuguese of Jewish descent, physician to Queen Elizabeth, accused of plotting against the life of Her Majesty and of the Pretender to the throne of Portugal, one Antonio. The trial of this Lopez aroused wild

popular excitement, fomented by Essex and his party. The
poor man was tried in the Guildhall, Essex presiding; he
was condemned; hanged, drawn and quartered in June,
1594. Sir Sidney Lee was the first to suggest this Lopez
as the original of Shylock. Dr Furness has followed up
this suggestion in his *Variorum* edition; and the textual
editor (see note on copy, p. 117) has added further
confirmation by pointing out the pun on Lopez = Lupus
= Wolf in Gratiano's address to Shylock:

> thy currish spirit
> Governed a Wolf, who hanged for human slaughter,
> Even from the gallows did his fell soul fleet,
> And whilst thou layest in thy unhallowed dam,
> Infused itself in thee; for thy desires
> Are wolvish, bloody, starved, and ravenous.

On all this we have here but three remarks to make.

In the first place, Gratiano's words may easily have
been an interpolation by an actor making a topical hit
after June, 1594; or indeed, Shakespeare may possibly
have been responsible for the insertion. He was after
all a working dramatist, and we know that he often
played up to his audience while despising himself for
doing so.

> Alas, 'tis true I have gone here and there
> And made myself a motley to the view,
> Gored mine own thoughts, sold cheap what is most dear,
> Made old offences of affections new.

In the second place it is just possible but no more than
this that early in 1594 and before this interpolation
Shakespeare was pleading very subtly for mercy on this
man. It is observable that all Portia's pleas addressed to
Shylock are Christian pleas, with which a Christian
audience might be expected to sympathise, certainly not
the Hebrew she addresses. This however can lead only
to speculation. What concerns us is that Shakespeare
had a chord in him which vibrated to music whenever

he appealed to mercy as divinely tempering justice. Hear, for instance, Isabella in *Measure for Measure*:

> *Angelo.* Your brother is a forfeit of the law,
> And you but waste your words.
>   *Isabella.*   Alas, alas...
> Why, all the souls that were were forfeit once,
> And He that might the vantage best have took
> Found out the remedy: how would you be,
> If He, which is the top of judgement, should
> But judge you, as you are?

But, most important of all, Lopez was a particular man, and died long ago. Whatever kind of man he was, he was not Shylock, who is an immortal universal creation and lives yet.

VI

Now for the individual Shylock, who in our opinion has been over-philosophised and over-sentimentalised, we may start upon the simple, obvious text that Shakespeare (who, in an age when Jews were forbidden this country, had probably never met with one in the flesh) makes him an intelligible if not a pardonable man; a genuine man, at any rate, of like passions with ourselves, so that we respond to every word of his fierce protest:

Hath not a Jew eyes? hath not a Jew hands, organs, dimensions, senses, affections, passions? fed with the same food, hurt with the same weapons, subject to the same diseases, healed by the same means, warmed and cooled by the same winter and summer, as a Christian is?

—makes him entirely more human than the conventional Jew of *Il Pecorone* or than the magniloquent monster created by Marlowe—makes him, up to the moment of his defeat by a woman's art, the tall dominating man of the play, tall as Coriolanus and nearer to us than Coriolanus in his scorn, sense of injury and motive of revenge. That Shakespeare knew Marlowe's play well seems a certain supposition, even if he had not so plainly 'bor-

rowed' Marlowe's *scène à faire* in which Abigail lowers
the treasure to her father from the convent window[1].
The 'alternative' sentences, too, pronounced in the
end upon Barabas and upon Shylock, with the choice
allowed, surely suggest imitation. But, anyhow, Shakespeare must have been well acquainted with Marlowe's
play.

How, then, does Shakespeare do it?—how contrive
to make Shylock sympathetic to us as Barabas never is?
Well, Marlowe's Jew, as Shakespeare's, has one only
daughter who is the apple of his eye: and this Jew with
one only daughter, ancient as balladry and repeated in
Ivanhoe by Scott, whom we always find intimate in,
not merely with, Shakespeare. His Isaac the Jew had
one fair daughter, as had Jephthah according to Hamlet[2].

But here Shakespeare comes in. His audience, con-
ventionally minded, may accept the proffer of the bond
(Act 1, Scene 3) as a jesting bargain made with blood-
thirsty intent, to be blood-thirstily enacted; but a gentle
Shakespeare cannot. There must be more incentive to
hate, to lust for a literally bloody vengeance, than any
past insults, however conventional, put upon him on the
Rialto by Antonio, mildest of men, can dramatically
supply. Sufferance is the badge of his tribe.

But he is a fierce Israelite and has an adored daughter.
In the interim between the signing of the bond and its
falling due this daughter, this Jessica, has wickedly and
most unfilially betrayed him. Abigail in *The Jew of
Malta* is a good girl, a true staunch daughter until she

---

[1] For this scene, and for once, Shakespeare borrowed
without improving. There is in *The Jew of Malta* a real
reason for this stealthy transportation. There is none in
The Merchant. Jessica, already dressed for flight, might
even just have walked downstairs and handed the money-
bags to her lover.

[2] And we know now that Hamlet was jigging upon an
actual ballad.

learns that her father has coldly contrived to murder the man to whom she has given her heart. For her father's sake she becomes a pretended convertite and salves his hidden treasure. Later, when convinced that he has compassed her lover's destruction, she becomes a genuine convertite: but remains so true a daughter that she cannot expose her father's villainy. It is upon a wrong suspicion that he curses and poisons her with the whole nunnery: and so in Marlowe's play Barabas tails off from grand promise into a mere villain—despite all further sonority on the old trick—an abject, unmeet for human concern, almost a ghastly figure of fun.

Shakespeare makes other play with Shylock. The Jew of Malta's daughter was loyal and good: but Jessica is bad and disloyal, unfilial, a thief; frivolous, greedy, without any more conscience than a cat and without even a cat's redeeming love of home. Quite without heart, on worse than an animal instinct—pilfering to be carnal —she betrays her father to be a light-of-lucre carefully weighted with her sire's ducats. So Shylock returns from a gay abhorrent banquet to knock on his empty and emptied house.

In stories of Jewry, even when told by the Jews themselves, it is always a difficult business to separate out (*a*) racial pride, (*b*) intense family affection, and (*c*) lucre. No one, on the other hand, reading the *Paston Letters* can fail to see that marriage between English families in the fifteenth century was ordinarily a matter of prepared commercial arrangement. Quite apart from race we may say that matrimony down to Shakespeare's time was accepted among parents as very much more of a trade—of hard business—than our modern sentiment admits it, at all events openly, to be. But the racial pride of Shylock has fenced off his daughter fiercely from any intercourse whatever with the infidels: and her elopement with one of the most heartless fribblers on the list of Antonio's friends, which is to say much, and the 'gilding' of herself, as on an afterthought, with more of her father's ducats before she runs downstairs to the street, leaves us with no alternative. Shylock is intolerably wronged.

VII[1]

Let us turn aside for a moment to Antonio, and to consider his friends and associates taken as a lot. It may not be always true that a man is known by the company he keeps: and most of us have known some man or two or three, of probity and high intellectual gifts, who are never at ease save in company with their moral and intellectual inferiors, avoid their peers, and of indolence consort with creatures among whom their eminence cannot be challenged. Such a man is Antonio, presented to us as a high-minded and capable merchant of credit and renown, but presented to us also as the indolent patron of a circle of wasters, 'born to consume the fruits of this world,' heartless, or at least unheedful, while his life lies in jeopardy through his tender, extravagantly romantic friendship for one of them.

Now it may be that Shakespeare, in the first half of this play purposely, of his art, hardened down all these friends and clients of the Merchant. Even as in *Macbeth* he afterwards helped to throw up his two protagonists by flattening down (the honest, thinking Banquo once removed) all the subordinate persons into mere figures of tapestry. And, if intended, this disheartening of Venice does indeed help to throw up Shylock with his passion into high relief.

But, if so, surely it is done at great cost. It has happened to us (say) to have read or witnessed *The*

---

[1] Portions of this section, together with a few passages in sections VIII and IX, are taken, by kind permission of Mr T. Fisher Unwin, from *Shakespeare's Workmanship* (1918), a volume of lectures given at Cambridge.

Merchant of Venice next after *As You Like It*; to have
overed a stile on the fringe of Arden,

> So frolic, so gay, and so green, so green, so green

—so, so fantastically English and so heartsome withal—
and step straight out of our native woodlands into the
most romantic of Italian cities—steeped in romance she
lies before us, sea-cradled, resplendent under southern
sunshine. We are in Venice—with all Vanity Fair, all
the *Carnival de Venise*, in full swing on her quays;
grave merchants trafficking, porters sweating with bales,
water-carriers, flower-girls, gallants; vessels lading, dis-
charging, repairing; and up the narrower waterways
black gondolas shooting under high guarded windows,
any gondola you please hooding a secret of love, or
assassination, or both—as any shutter in the line may
open demurely, discreetly, giving just room enough,
just time enough, for a hand to drop a rose. Venice
again at night—lanterns on the water, masked revellers
taking charge of the quays with drums, hautboys, fifes,
and general tipsiness; withdrawn from this riot into deep
intricacies of shadow, the undertone of lutes complaining their love; and out beyond all this fever, far
to southward, the stars swinging, keeping their circle
—as Queen Elizabeth once danced—'high and dis-
posedly' over Belmont, where on a turfed bank

> Peace, ho! the moon sleeps with Endymion,
> And would not be awaked,

though the birds have already begun to twitter in Portia's
garden. Have we not here the very atmosphere of
romance?

Well, no....We have a perfect *setting* for romance;
but setting and atmosphere are two very different things.
Chaucer will take a tale of Boccaccio's and in the telling
alter its atmosphere wholly: the reason being that while
setting is external, atmosphere emanates from the author's
genius, is breathed out from within.

Now in the *Merchant of Venice*, barring the Merchant himself, a merely static figure, and Shylock, who is meant to be cruel, every one of the Venetian *dramatis personae* is either a 'waster' or a 'rotter' or both, and cold-hearted at that. There is no need to expend ink upon such parasites as surround Antonio—upon Salerio and Solanio. Be it granted that in the hour of his extremity they have no means to save him. Yet they see it coming; they discuss it sympathetically, but always on the assumption that it is his affair not theirs:

> Let good Antonio look he keep his day,
> Or he shall pay for this,

and they take not so much trouble as to send Bassanio word of his friend's plight, though they know that for Bassanio's sake his deadly peril has been incurred! It is left to Antonio himself to tell the news in that very noble letter of farewell and release:

Sweet Bassanio, my ships have all miscarried, my creditors grow cruel, my estate is very low, my bond to the Jew is forfeit, and since, in paying it, it is impossible I should live, all debts are cleared between you and I, if I might but see you at my death: notwithstanding, use your pleasure—if your love do not persuade you to come, let not my letter

—a letter which, in good truth, Bassanio does not too extravagantly describe as 'a few of the unpleasant'st words that ever blotted paper.' Let us compare it with Salerio's account of how the friends had parted:

> I saw Bassanio and Antonio part.
> Bassanio told him he would make some speed
> Of his return: he answered, 'Do not so.
> Slubber not business for my sake, Bassanio,
> But stay the very riping of the time.
> And for the Jew's bond which he hath of me,
> Let it not enter in your mind of love:
> Be merry, and employ your chiefest thoughts
> To courtship, and such fair ostents of love
> As shall conveniently become you there.'
> And even there, his eye being big with tears,

> Turning his face, he put his hand behind him,
> And with affection wondrous sensible
> He wrung Bassanio's hand, and so they parted.

But let us consider this conquering hero, Bassanio. When we first meet him he is in debt, a condition on which—having to confess it because he wants to borrow more money—he expends some very choice diction.

> 'Tis not unknown to you, Antonio,

(No, it certainly was not!)

> How much I have disabled mine estate,
> By something showing a more swelling port
> Than my faint means would grant continuance.

That may be a mighty fine way of saying that you have chosen to live beyond your income; but, Shakespeare or no Shakespeare, if Shakespeare mean us to hold Bassanio for an honest fellow, it is mighty poor poetry. For poetry, like honest men, looks things in the face, and does not ransack its wardrobe to clothe what is naturally unpoetical. Bassanio, to do him justice, is not trying to wheedle Antonio by this sort of talk; he knows his friend too deeply for that. But he is deceiving *himself*, or rather is reproducing some of the trash with which he has already deceived himself.

He goes on to say that he is not repining; his chief anxiety is to pay everybody, and

> To you, Antonio,
> I owe the most in money and in love,

and thereupon counts on more love to extract more money, starting (and upon an experienced man of business, be it observed) with some windy nonsense about shooting a second arrow after a lost one.

> You know me well, and herein spend but time
> To wind about my love with circumstance

says Antonio; and, indeed, his gentle impatience throughout this scene is well worth noting. He is friend enough already to give all; but to be preached at, and on a subject—money—of which he has forgotten, or chooses to forget, ten times more than Bassanio will ever learn, is a little beyond bearing. And what is Bassanio's project? To borrow three thousand ducats to equip himself to go off and hunt an heiress in Belmont. He has seen her; she is fair; and

> sometimes from her eyes
> I did receive fair speechless messages....
> Nor is the wide world ignorant of her worth,
> For the four winds blow in from every coast
> Renownéd suitors, and her sunny locks
> Hang on her temples like a golden fleece,
> Which makes her seat of Belmont Colchos' strand,
> And many Jasons come in quest of her....
> O my Antonio, had I but the means
> To hold a rival place with one of them,
> I have a mind presages me such thrift,
> That I should questionless be fortunate.

Now this is bad workmanship and dishonouring to Bassanio. It suggests the obvious question, Why should he build anything on Portia's encouraging glances, as why should he 'questionless be fortunate,' seeing that —as he knows perfectly well, but does not choose to confide to the friend whose money he is borrowing— Portia's glances, encouraging or not, are nothing to the purpose, since all depends on his choosing the right one of three caskets—a two to one chance against him?

But he gets the money, of course, equips himself lavishly, arrives at Belmont; and here comes in worse workmanship. For I suppose that, while character weighs in drama, if one thing be more certain than another it is that a predatory young gentleman such as Bassanio would *not* have chosen the leaden casket. Let us consider his soliloquy while choosing:

> The world is still deceived with ornament.
> In law, what plea so tainted and corrupt,
> But, being seasoned with a gracious voice,
> Obscures the show of evil? In religion,

> What damnéd error, but some sober brow
> Will bless it, and approve it with a text.

One feels moved to interrupt: 'Yes, yes—and what about yourself, my little fellow? What has altered you, that you, of all men, suddenly use this sanctimonious talk?'

And this flaw in characterisation goes right down through the workmanship of the play. For the evil opposed against these curious Christians is specific; it is Cruelty; and, yet again specifically, the peculiar cruelty of a Jew. To this cruelty an artist at the top of his art would surely have opposed mansuetude, clemency, charity, and, specifically, Christian charity. Shakespeare misses more than half the point when he makes the intended victims, as a class and by habit, just as heartless as Shylock without any of Shylock's passionate excuse.

So from these Venetians we return to Shylock. He has, one must repeat, been over-sentimentalised and over-philosophised. Macklin or Charles Kean began it on the stage, and Irving completed what they began. But in literature we find it already running strong in Heine, himself a Jew. He tells how in a box at Drury Lane he sat next to 'a pale, fair Briton who at the end of the Fourth Act fell a-weeping passionately, several times exclaiming "the poor man is wronged!"' and Heine goes on to return the compliment in better coin with talk about 'a ripple of tears that were never wept by eyes...a sob that could come only from a breast that held in it the martyrdom endured for eighteen centuries by a whole tortured people.'

At this point it may be salutary to oppose sense to sensibility by quoting some less sympathetic observations by James Spedding.

The best contribution I can offer to this discussion is the expression of an old man's difficulty in accepting these new discoveries of profound moral and political designs underlying Shakespeare's choice and treatment of his subjects: I believe that he was a man of business,—that his principal business was to produce plays which would draw. I believe that he took the story of the caskets and of the pound of flesh because he thought he could combine them...into a good romantic comedy that was likely to succeed; and I think he managed it very well. But if, instead of looking about for a story to 'please' the Globe audience, he had been in search of a subject under cover of which he might steal into their minds 'a more tolerant feeling towards the Hebrew race,' I cannot think he would have selected for his hero a rich Jewish merchant plotting the murder of a Christian rival by means of a fraudulent contract, which made death the penalty of non-payment at the day, and insisting on the exaction of it. In a modern Christian audience it seems to be possible for a skilful actor to work on the feelings of an audience so far as to make a man engaged in such a business an object of respectful sympathy. But can anybody believe that, in times when this would have been much more difficult, Shakespeare would have *chosen* such a case as a favourable one to suggest toleration to a public prejudiced against Jews? A lawyer retained to defend a man who has kicked his wife to death will try to prove that his client was an injured husband, and had served her right, and this may succeed with a jury that have had experience of conjugal provocations. But if his business were to plead for a mitigation of the severity of the law *against husbands*, he would surely keep his injured friend's case as far out of sight as he could. I do not believe, in fact, that Shakespeare, either in choosing the subject or treating it, was thinking about Jewish grievances or disabilities at all either way. What he had to think about was, how he could introduce into a *comedy*, without putting everything out of tune, an incident so shocking, and a project so savage, that 'the imagination almost refuses to approach it.' And I think he managed this also very skilfully, by first depriving Shylock of all pretence of grievance or excuse, which was done by the offer of all the money due to him upon his bond, with twice as much more to compensate him for the very short time he had had to wait for it beyond the appointed day,—an offer which leaves him without any conceivable motive for preferring the pound of flesh except the worst,— and then dismissing him with a punishment very much lighter than he deserved.

As the reader will have seen, we cannot agree with Spedding that Shakespeare deprived Shylock 'of all pretence of grievance or excuse.' On the contrary, we hold that in the abduction of Jessica Shakespeare deliberately gives him a real grievance and excuse, and that the offer of money, belatedly made, comes almost as an insult to his passionate resentment.

But surely, as these philosophers overlook, and as every author and every intelligent reader should know, how apt is creative genius to be carried away by a character it creates. Few of us doubt Spedding's assertion that Shakespeare intended to make Shylock such a cruel, crafty, villainous Hebrew as would appeal to an audience of Elizabethan Christians. The very structure of the plot shows this. But even as Don Quixote carried away Cervantes, and Pickwick Dickens, so Shylock takes charge of Shakespeare, no less imperiously than Falstaff took charge of him. The intelligence of his heart and springs of action once admitted, Shakespeare understands him in detail, down (as Hazlitt noted) to his Biblical language, as when he hears that Jessica has given in Genoa a ring to purchase a monkey, he breaks out with: 'Thou torturest me, Tubal—it was my turquoise— I had it of Leah when I was a bachelor: I would not have given it for a wilderness of monkeys.'

VIII

We turn from Shylock to his antagonist, Portia, of whom in our opinion the critics in general have made too little. They have made, indeed, too much of her in the trial-scene, so that we usually picture her to ourselves as the slim figure of that scene dressed in doctor's robes: and this no doubt was in Hazlitt's mind, who found her something of a pedant. Something of a pedant in those surroundings she had to be, or pretend to be. But her real charm may be better studied in Acts 3 and 5.

Let us turn for instance from the trial-scene to her lovely confession:

> You see me, Lord Bassanio, where I stand,
> Such as I am; though for myself alone
> I would not be ambitious in my wish
> To wish myself much better, yet for you
> I would be trebled twenty times myself—
> A thousand times more fair, ten thousand times
> More rich—
> That only to stand high in your account,
> I might in virtues, beauties, livings, friends,
> Exceed account: but the full sum of me
> Is some of something...which, to term in gross,
> Is an unlessoned girl, unschooled, unpractised,
> Happy in this, she is not yet so old
> But she may learn; happier than this,
> She is not bred so dull but she can learn;
> Happiest of all is that her gentle spirit
> Commits itself to yours to be directed,
> As from her lord, her governor, her king....
> Myself and what is mine to you and yours
> Is now converted....But now I was the lord
> Of this fair mansion, master of my servants,
> Queen o'er myself; and even now, but now,
> This house, these servants, and this same myself,
> Are yours—my lord's!—I give them with this ring.

We are a long way here from the lady in *Il Pecorone*, who, as we saw, is a descendant of Circe and the Laidly Worm. Nor is Portia transformed by a kiss. Like the Merchant, she is good throughout, although like the Merchant wistful in the opening scene, as Croce notes:

'By my troth, Nerissa, my little body is aweary of this great world' (she sighs, with gentle coquetry towards herself), perhaps with that languor, which is the desire of loving and of being loved, the budding of love; weary, as those amorous souls feel weary, who vibrate with an exquisite sensibility.

Shakespeare, of course, in working this opening scene exhibits his usual economy in borrowing from himself, the discussion of the suitors between Portia and Nerissa being but an improvement on Julia's talk with Lucetta in the *Two Gentlemen of Verona*, even as Portia's assumption of male attire later in the play is an improvement on Julia's. She is already at least well disposed to the youthful Venetian, something between a student and a soldier, half an adventurer, but courteous and pleasing in address, who has contrived to please not only mistress but maid, which shows, in this agreement of feminine choice, where feminine taste really lies.

It is perhaps fanciful, perhaps also mischievous, to suggest that whether by invention of mistress or maid, the words sung to music while Bassanio prepares to make his choice give it a hint of guidance[1]. We may note at least that the first three lines—

> Tell me where is Fancy bred,
> Or in the heart, or in the head?
> How begot, how nourishéd?—

rhyme with *lead*, and surely when Fancy dies in the cradle where it lies there may be a hint of the leaden coffin in which Love lies lapped in lead like King Pandion and all the friends of Philomel.

Yet, as Portia says, 'Tarry a little, there is something else.' One would like to believe that against Venice with its moral emptiness, Shakespeare consciously and deliberately opposed Belmont (the Hill Beautiful) as the residence of that better part of the Renaissance, its 'humanities,' its adoration of beauty, its wistful dream of a golden age. It is, at any rate, observable in the play that—whether under the spell of Portia or from some other cause—nobody arrives at Belmont who is not instantly and marvellously the better for it; and this is no less true of Bassanio than of Lorenzo and Jessica and Gratiano. All the suitors, be it remarked—Morocco and Arragon no less than Bassanio—address themselves

---

[1] v. note 3. 2. 63–72.

nobly to the trial and take their fate nobly. If this be
what Shakespeare meant by Belmont, we can read a
great deal into Portia's first words to Nerissa in Act 5
as, reaching home again, she emerges on the edge of the
dark shrubbery:

> That light we see is burning in my hall...
> How far that little candle throws his beams!
> So shines a good deed in a naughty world

—a *naughty* world: a world that is naught, having no
heart.

IX

This leads naturally to a consideration of the Fifth
Act, which has been amazingly underrated by the
critics, many of whom do not seem to understand the
value of 'the falling close' in poetry. We have seen that
up to a certain point in Act 4 *The Merchant of Venice*
moves towards Tragedy, and this movement is arrested
only by Portia's challenge—'Why doth the Jew pause?'
By that challenge Antonio's life is saved; none the less
the close of the Act leaves us in the surcharged atmosphere
of a court of justice. The Fifth Act redeems us into a
world in which good folk are happy with free hearts
that move to music, without an understanding of which
a man is fit only for treasons, stratagems and spoils. We
have to be won back to a saner, happier acceptance of
life; and so we are, by gracious, most playful comedy.
It is all absurd, if we please. The unsealing of a letter
telling Antonio, to make joy complete, that

> three of your argosies
> Are richly come to harbour suddenly

is unbelievable. 'You shall not know,' Portia adds,

> You shall not know by what strange accident
> I chancéd on this letter.

No, nor anyone else! It is as absurd as the conclusion of
The Vicar of Wakefield. Yet it is not more absurd than
the huddled ending of many an Elizabethan play—of

The Alchemist, for instance, or of *The White Devil,* or the last scene of *Cymbeline* where curiosity has counted for us no less than twenty-four cumulated *dénouements* within the compass of 455 lines.

It is fairly evident that Shakespeare made at least one attempt at it before satisfying himself; as plain as that, if we resolutely hold the trial-scene back to focus, this finish becomes the most delightful Act in the play.

That Shakespeare tried other ways is made evident by one line. Upon Lorenzo's and Jessica's lovely duet there breaks a footfall. Lorenzo, startled by it, demands:

Lorenzo. Who comes so fast in silence of the night?
Stephano. A friend.
Lorenzo. A friend! what friend? your name, I pray you, friend?
Stephano. Stephano is my name, and I bring word
My mistress will before the break of day
Be here at Belmont—she doth stray about
By holy crosses, where she kneels and prays
For happy wedlock hours.
Lorenzo.   Who comes with her?
Stephano. None, but a holy hermit, and her maid....

Nothing loose in literature—in play or in poem—ever caught Dr Johnson napping. 'I do not perceive,' says Johnson, in his unfaltering accent, 'the use of this hermit, of whom nothing is seen or heard afterwards. The Poet had first planned his fable some other way; and inadvertently, when he changed his scheme, retained something of the original design.'

And while all this has been passing, the moon has sunk and every thicket around Belmont has begun to thrill and sing of dawn. Portia lifts a hand:

> It is almost morning,
> Let us go in.

And so the comedy comes home. 'Pack, clouds, away! and welcome, day!'

[1926]   Q.

TO THE READER

The following is a brief description of the punctuation and other typographical devices employed in the text, which have been more fully explained in the *Note on Punctuation* and the *Textual Introduction* to be found in *The Tempest* volume:

An obelisk (†) implies corruption or emendation, and suggests a reference to the Notes.

A single bracket at the beginning of a speech signifies an 'aside.'

The reference number for the first line is given at the head of each page. Numerals in square brackets are placed at the beginning of the traditional acts and scenes.

The most excellent
Historie of the *Merchant*
of Venice.

VVith the extreame crueltie of *Shylocke* the Iewe
towards the sayd Merchant, in cutting a iust pound
of his flesh: and the obtayning of *Portia*
by the choyse of three
chests.

As it hath beene diuers times acted by the Lord
Chamberlaine his Seruants.

Written by William Shakespeare.

AT LONDON,
Printed by *I. R.* for Thomas Heyes,
and are to be sold in Paules Church-yard, at the
signe of the Greene Dragon.
1600.

4

The scene Venice, and
Portia's house at Belmont

CHARACTERS IN THE PLAY

The Duke of Venice

The Prince of Morocco
The Prince of Arragon
} *suitors to Portia*

ANTONIO, *a Merchant of Venice*

BASSANIO, *his friend, suitor to Portia*

GRATIANO
SOLANIO
SALERIO
} *friends to Antonio and Bassanio*

LORENZO, *in love with Jessica*

SHYLOCK, *a Jew*

TUBAL, *another Jew, friend to Shylock*

LANCELOT GOBBO, *a clown, servant to Shylock*

OLD GOBBO, *father to Lancelot*

LEONARDO, *servant to Bassanio*

BALTHAZAR
STEPHANO
} *servants to Portia*

PORTIA, *a lady of Belmont*

NERISSA, *her waiting-maid*

JESSICA, *daughter to Shylock*

*Magnificoes of Venice, officers of the Court of Justice,
a gaoler, servants, and other attendants*

THE MERCHANT OF VENICE

ANTONIO, SALERIO, and SOLANIO approach,
talking together

Antonio. In sooth I know not why I am so sad,
It wearies me, you say it wearies you;
But how I caught it, found it, or came by it,
What stuff 'tis made of, whereof it is born,
I am to learn:
And such a want-wit sadness makes of me,
That I have much ado to know myself.

Salerio. Your mind is tossing on the ocean,
There, where your argosies with portly sail—
Like signiors and rich burghers on the flood,   10
Or as it were the pageants of the sea—
Do overpeer the petty traffickers,
That curtsy to them, do them reverence,
As they fly by them with their woven wings.

Solanio. Believe me, sir, had I such venture forth,
The better part of my affections would
Be with my hopes abroad. I should be still
Plucking the grass to know where sits the wind,
Piring in maps for ports and piers and roads:
And every object that might make me fear   20
Misfortune to my ventures, out of doubt,
Would make me sad.

Salerio.   My wind, cooling my broth,
Would blow me to an ague when I thought
What harm a wind too great might do at sea.
I should not see the sandy hour-glass run
But I should think of shallows and of flats,

And see my wealthy Andrew docked in sand,
Vailing her high-top lower than her ribs
To kiss her burial...Should I go to church
30 And see the holy edifice of stone,
And not bethink me straight of dangerous rocks,
Which touching but my gentle vessel's side
Would scatter all her spices on the stream,
Enrobe the roaring waters with my silks,
And, in a word, but even now worth this,
And now worth nothing? Shall I have the thought
To think on this, and shall I lack the thought
That such a thing bechanced would make me sad?
But tell not me—I know Antonio
40 Is sad to think upon his merchandise.
  Antonio. Believe me, no—I thank my fortune for it—
My ventures are not in one bottom trusted,
Nor to one place; nor is my whole estate
Upon the fortune of this present year:
Therefore my merchandise makes me not sad.
  Solanio. Why then you are in love.
  Antonio.   Fie, fie!
  Solanio. Not in love neither? then let us say you are sad
Because you are not merry; and 'twere as easy
For you to laugh and leap, and say you are merry,
50 Because you are not sad. Now, by two-headed Janus,
Nature hath framed strange fellows in her time:
Some that will evermore peep through their eyes,
And laugh like parrots at a bag-piper;
And other of such vinegar aspect,
That they'll not show their teeth in way of smile,
Though Nestor swear the jest be laughable....

BASSANIO, LORENZO, and GRATIANO are seen approaching

Here comes Bassanio, your most noble kinsman,

Gratiano, and Lorenzo....Fare ye well,
We leave you now with better company.

Salerio. I would have stayed till I had made you merry, 60
If worthier friends had not prevented me.

Antonio. Your worth is very dear in my regard.
I take it your own business calls on you,
And you embrace th'occasion to depart.

Salerio. Good morrow, my good lords.

Bassanio [*coming up*]. Good signiors both, when shall
  we laugh? say when?
You grow exceeding strange: must it be so?

Salerio. We'll make our leisures to attend on yours.
                    [*Salerio and Solanio bow and depart*

Lorenzo. My Lord Bassanio, since you have
  found Antonio,
We two will leave you, but at dinner-time   70
I pray you have in mind where we must meet.

Bassanio. I will not fail you.

Gratiano. You look not well, Signior Antonio,
You have too much respect upon the world:
They lose it that do buy it with much care,
Believe me you are marvellously changed.

Antonio. I hold the world but as the world, Gratiano—
A stage, where every man must play a part,
And mine a sad one.

Gratiano.   Let me play the fool,
With mirth and laughter let old wrinkles come,   80
And let my liver rather heat with wine,
Than my heart cool with mortifying groans.
Why should a man, whose blood is warm within,
Sit like his grandsire cut in alabaster?
Sleep when he wakes? and creep into the jaundice
By being peevish? I tell thee what, Antonio—
I love thee, and it is my love that speaks—

There are a sort of men whose visages
Do cream and mantle like a standing pond,
90 And do a wilful stillness entertain,
With purpose to be dressed in an opinion
Of wisdom, gravity, profound conceit,
As who should say, 'I am Sir Oracle,
And when I ope my lips let no dog bark'....
O, my Antonio, I do know of these
That therefore only are reputed wise
For saying nothing...when, I am very sure,
If they should speak, would almost damn those ears
Which, hearing them, would call their brothers fools.
100 I'll tell thee more of this another time.
But fish not with this melancholy bait
For this fool gudgeon, this opinion...
Come, good Lorenzo. Fare ye well awhile,
I'll end my exhortation after dinner.
    Lorenzo. Well, we will leave you then till dinner-time.
I must be one of these same dumb wise men,
For Gratiano never lets me speak.
    Gratiano. Well, keep me company but two years mo,
Thou shalt not know the sound of thine own tongue.
110 *Antonio.* Fare you well. I'll grow a talker for
        this gear.
    Gratiano. Thanks, i'faith—for silence is only
        commendable
In a neat's tongue dried, and a maid not vendible.
        [*Gratiano and Lorenzo go off laughing, arm-in-arm*
    Antonio. Is that any thing now?
    Bassanio. Gratiano speaks an infinite deal of nothing,
more than any man in all Venice. His reasons are as
two grains of wheat hid in two bushels of chaff: you
shall seek all day ere you find them, and when you
have them they are not worth the search.

Antonio. Well, tell me now what lady is the same
To whom you swore a secret pilgrimage,   120
That you to-day promised to tell me of?
Bassanio. 'Tis not unknown to you, Antonio,
How much I have disabled mine estate,
By something showing a more swelling port
Than my faint means would grant continuance:
Nor do I now make moan to be abridged
From such a noble rate, but my chief care
Is to come fairly off from the great debts
Wherein my time, something too prodigal,
Hath left me gaged. To you, Antonio,   130
I owe the most in money and in love,
And from your love I have a warranty
To unburthen all my plots and purposes
How to get clear of all the debts I owe.
Antonio. I pray you, good Bassanio, let me know it,
And if it stand, as you yourself still do,
Within the eye of honour, be assured,
My purse, my person, my extremest means,
Lie all unlocked to your occasions.
Bassanio. In my school-days, when I had lost one shaft, 140
I shot his fellow of the self-same flight
The self-same way, with more adviséd watch,
To find the other forth, and by adventuring both,
I oft found both: I urge this childhood proof,
Because what follows is pure innocence....
I owe you much, and, like a wilful youth,
That which I owe is lost—but if you please
To shoot another arrow that self way
Which you did shoot the first, I do not doubt,
As I will watch the aim, or to find both,   150
Or bring your latter hazard back again,
And thankfully rest debtor for the first.

Antonio. You know me well, and herein spend but time
To wind about my love with circumstance,
And out of doubt you do me now more wrong
In making question of my uttermost
Than if you had made waste of all I have:
Then do but say to me what I should do
That in your knowledge may by me be done,
160 And I am prest unto it: therefore, speak.
  Bassanio. In Belmont is a lady richly left,
And she is fair, and, fairer than that word,
Of wondrous virtues—sometimes from her eyes
I did receive fair speechless messages.
Her name is Portia, nothing undervalued
To Cato's daughter, Brutus' Portia;
Nor is the wide world ignorant of her worth,
For the four winds blow in from every coast
Renownéd suitors, and her sunny locks
170 Hang on her temples like a golden fleece,
Which makes her seat of Belmont Colchos' strand,
And many Jasons come in quest of her.
O my Antonio, had I but the means
To hold a rival place with one of them,
I have a mind presages me such thrift,
That I should questionless be fortunate.
  Antonio. Thou know'st that all my fortunes are at sea,
Neither have I money nor commodity
To raise a present sum, therefore go forth,
180 Try what my credit can in Venice do—
That shall be racked, even to the uttermost,
To furnish thee to Belmont, to fair Portia.
Go, presently inquire, and so will I,
Where money is, and I no question make
To have it of my trust or for my sake.   [*they go*

[1.2.] *The hall of Portia's house at Belmont; at the back a gallery and beneath it the entrance to an alcove concealed by a curtain*

PORTIA *and her waiting-woman* NERISSA

Portia. By my troth, Nerissa, my little body is aweary of this great world.

Nerissa. You would be, sweet madam, if your miseries were in the same abundance as your good fortunes are: and yet for aught I see, they are as sick that surfeit with too much as they that starve with nothing; it is no mean happiness therefore to be seated in the mean—superfluity comes sooner by white hairs, but competency lives longer.

Portia. Good sentences, and well pronounced.

Nerissa. They would be better if well followed.   10

Portia. If to do were as easy as to know what were good to do, chapels had been churches, and poor men's cottages princes' palaces. It is a good divine that follows his own instructions. I can easier teach twenty what were good to be done, than be one of the twenty to follow mine own teaching...The brain may devise laws for the blood, but a hot temper leaps o'er a cold decree—such a hare is madness the youth, to skip o'er the meshes of good counsel the cripple...But this reasoning is not in the fashion to choose me a husband. 20 O me, the word 'choose'! I may neither choose whom I would nor refuse whom I dislike—so is the will of a living daughter curbed by the will of a dead father... Is it not hard, Nerissa, that I cannot choose one, nor refuse none?

Nerissa. Your father was ever virtuous, and holy men at their death have good inspirations, therefore the lottery that he hath devised in these three chests of gold, silver and lead, whereof who chooses his meaning

30 chooses you, will no doubt never be chosen by any
rightly, but one whom you shall rightly love. But what
warmth is there in your affection towards any of these
princely suitors that are already come?

Portia. I pray thee over-name them, and as thou
namest them, I will describe them, and according to my
description level at my affection.

Nerissa. First there is the Neapolitan prince.

Portia. Ay, that's a colt indeed, for he doth nothing
but talk of his horse, and he makes it a great appropria-
40 tion to his own good parts that he can shoe him himself:
I am much afeard my lady his mother played false
with a smith.

Nerissa. Then is there the County Palatine.

Portia. He doth nothing but frown, as who should
say, 'An you will not have me, choose!' He hears
merry tales, and smiles not. I fear he will prove the
weeping philosopher when he grows old, being so full
of unmannerly sadness in his youth. I had rather be
married to a death's-head with a bone in his mouth
50 than to either of these: God defend me from these two!

Nerissa. How say you by the French lord, Monsieur
Le Bon?

Portia. God made him, and therefore let him pass
for a man—In truth, I know it is a sin to be a mocker,
but he! why, he hath a horse better than the Neapolitan's, a better bad habit of frowning than the Count
Palatine—he is every man in no man—if a throstle sing,
he falls straight a cap'ring—he will fence with his own
shadow. If I should marry him, I should marry twenty
60 husbands. If he would despise me I would forgive him,
for if he love me to madness, I shall never requite him.

Nerissa. What say you then to Falconbridge, the
young baron of England?

Portia. You know I say nothing to him, for he understands not me, nor I him: he hath neither Latin, French, nor Italian, and you will come into the court and swear that I have a poor pennyworth in the English. He is a proper man's picture, but, alas! who can converse with a dumb-show? How oddly he is suited! I think he bought his doublet in Italy, his round hose in France, 70 his bonnet in Germany, and his behaviour every where.

Nerissa. What think you of the Scottish lord, his neighbour?

Portia. That he hath a neighbourly charity in him, for he borrowed a box of the ear of the Englishman, and swore he would pay him again when he was able: I think the Frenchman became his surety, and sealed under for another.

Nerissa. How like you the young German, the Duke of Saxony's nephew? 80

Portia. Very vilely in the morning when he is sober, and most vilely in the afternoon when he is drunk: when he is best, he is a little worse than a man, and when he is worst, he is little better than a beast. An the worst fall that ever fell, I hope I shall make shift to go without him.

Nerissa. If he should offer to choose, and choose the right casket, you should refuse to perform your father's will, if you should refuse to accept him.

Portia. Therefore, for fear of the worst, I pray thee 90 set a deep glass of rhenish wine on the contrary casket, for if the devil be within, and that temptation without, I know he will choose it. I will do any thing, Nerissa, ere I will be married to a sponge.

Nerissa. You need not fear, lady, the having any of these lords—they have acquainted me with their determinations, which is indeed to return to their home, and

to trouble you with no more suit, unless you may be
won by some other sort than your father's imposition
100 depending on the caskets.

Portia. If I live to be as old as Sibylla, I will die as
chaste as Diana, unless I be obtained by the manner of
my father's will. I am glad this parcel of wooers are
so reasonable, for there is not one among them but I
dote on his very absence: and I pray God grant them
a fair departure.

Nerissa. Do you not remember, lady, in your father's
time, a Venetian, a scholar and a soldier, that came
hither in company of the Marquis of Montferrat?

110 *Portia.* Yes, yes, it was Bassanio, as I think so was
he called.

Nerissa. True, madam, he, of all the men that ever
my foolish eyes looked upon, was the best deserving
a fair lady.

Portia. I remember him well, and I remember him
worthy of thy praise.

A servant enters

How now! what news?

Servant. The four strangers seek for you, madam, to
take their leave: and there is a forerunner come from
120 a fifth, the Prince of Morocco, who brings word the
prince his master will be here to-night.

Portia. If I could bid the fifth welcome with so good
heart as I can bid the other four farewell, I should be
glad of his approach: if he have the condition of a saint,
and the complexion of a devil, I had rather he should
shrive me than wive me.
Come, Nerissa. Sirrah, go before:
Whiles we shut the gate upon one wooer, another
              knocks at the door.   [*they go out*

[1.3.] *A street in Venice, before Shylock's house*

BASSANIO *and* SHYLOCK

Shylock. Three thousand ducats—well.

Bassanio. Ay, sir, for three months.

Shylock. For three months—well.

Bassanio. For the which, as I told you, Antonio shall be bound.

Shylock. Antonio shall become bound—well.

Bassanio. May you stead me? Will you pleasure me? Shall I know your answer?

Shylock. Three thousand ducats for three months— and Antonio bound.   10

Bassanio. Your answer to that.

Shylock. Antonio is a good man.

Bassanio. Have you heard any imputation to the contrary?

Shylock. Ho no, no, no, no...my meaning in saying he is a good man, is to have you understand me that he is sufficient. Yet his means are in supposition: he hath an argosy bound to Tripolis, another to the Indies; I understand moreover upon the Rialto, he hath a third at Mexico, a fourth for England, and other ventures he 20 hath squandered abroad. But ships are but boards, sailors but men—there be land-rats and water-rats, land-thieves and water-thieves—I mean pirates—and then there is the peril of waters, winds, and rocks. The man is, notwithstanding, sufficient. Three thousand ducats—I think I may take his bond.

Bassanio. Be assured you may.

Shylock. I will be assured I may: and, that I may be assured, I will bethink me—may I speak with Antonio?

Bassanio. If it please you to dine with us.   30

(Shylock. Yes, to smell pork, to eat of the habitation

which your prophet the Nazarite conjured the devil
into! I will buy with you, sell with you, talk with you,
walk with you, and so following: but I will not eat with
you, drink with you, nor pray with you....[*aloud*] What
news on the Rialto? Who is he comes here?

ANTONIO approaches

Bassanio. This is Signior Antonio.
> [*he draws Antonio aside*

(*Shylock*. How like a fawning publican he looks!
I hate him for he is a Christian:
40 But more for that in low simplicity
He lends out money gratis, and brings down
The rate of usance here with us in Venice.
If I can catch him once upon the hip,
I will feed fat the ancient grudge I bear him.
He hates our sacred nation, and he rails,
Even there where merchants most do congregate,
On me, my bargains, and my well-won thrift,
Which he calls interest. Cursèd be my tribe,
If I forgive him!
  Bassanio [*turns*]. Shylock, do you hear?
50 *Shylock*. I am debating of my present store,
And by the near guess of my memory
I cannot instantly raise up the gross
Of full three thousand ducats: what of that?
Tubal a wealthy Hebrew of my tribe
Will furnish me; but soft—how many months
Do you desire? [*bows to Antonio*] Rest you fair, good
    signior,
Your worship was the last man in our mouths.
  Antonio. Shylock, albeit I neither lend nor borrow
By taking nor by giving of excess,
60 Yet to supply the ripe wants of my friend

I'll break a custom...[*to Bassanio*] Is he yet possessed
How much ye would?

  Shylock.   Ay, ay, three thousand ducats.

  Antonio. And for three months.   65

  Shylock. I had forgot—three months—you told me so.
Well then, your bond: and let me see—but hear you,
Methoughts you said you neither lend nor borrow
Upon advantage.

  Antonio.   I do never use it.

  Shylock. When Jacob grazed his uncle Laban's sheep,
This Jacob from our holy Abram was
(As his wise mother wrought in his behalf)   70
The third possessor; ay, he was the third—

  Antonio. And what of him? did he take interest?

  Shylock. No, not take interest—not as you would say
Directly interest. Mark what Jacob did.
When Laban and himself were compromised
That all the eanlings which were streaked and pied
Should fall as Jacob's hire, the ewes, being rank
In end of autumn, turnéd to the rams,
And when the work of generation was
Between these woolly breeders in the act,   80
The skilful shepherd pilled me certain wands,
And, in the doing of the deed of kind,
He stuck them up before the fulsome ewes,
Who, then conceiving, did in eaning time
Fall parti-coloured lambs, and those were Jacob's.
This was a way to thrive, and he was blest:
And thrift is blessing if men steal it not.

  Antonio. This was a venture, sir, that Jacob served for—
A thing not in his power to bring to pass,
But swayed and fashioned by the hand of heaven. 90
Was this inserted to make interest good?
Or is your gold and silver ewes and rams?

Shylock. I cannot tell, I make it breed as fast!
But note me, signior.

Antonio. Mark you this, Bassanio,
The devil can cite Scripture for his purpose.
An evil soul, producing holy witness,
Is like a villain with a smiling cheek,
A goodly apple rotten at the heart.
O, what a goodly outside falsehood hath!

100 *Shylock.* Three thousand ducats—'tis a good
round sum.
Three months from twelve, then let me see the rate.

Antonio. Well, Shylock, shall we be beholding to you?

Shylock. Signior Antonio, many a time and oft
In the Rialto you have rated me
About my moneys and my usances:
Still have I borne it with a patient shrug,
For suff'rance is the badge of all our tribe.
You call me misbeliever, cut-throat dog,
And spit upon my Jewish gaberdine,

110 And all for use of that which is mine own.
Well then, it now appears you need my help:
Go to then, you come to me, and you say,
'Shylock, we would have moneys'—you say so!
You that did void your rheum upon my beard,
And foot me as you spurn a stranger cur
Over your threshold. Moneys is your suit.
What should I say to you? Should I not say
'Hath a dog money? is it possible
A cur can lend three thousand ducats?' or

120 Shall I bend low, and in a bondman's key,
With bated breath, and whisp'ring humbleness,
Say this:
'Fair sir, you spit on me on Wednesday last—
You spurned me such a day—another time

You called me dog: and for these courtesies
I'll lend you thus much moneys'?
  Antonio. I am as like to call thee so again,
To spit on thee again, to spurn thee too.
If thou wilt lend this money, lend it not
As to thy friends—for when did friendship take   130
A breed for barren metal of his friend?—
But lend it rather to thine enemy,
Who if he break, thou mayst with better face
Exact the penalty.
  Shylock.   Why, look you, how you storm!
I would be friends with you, and have your love,
Forget the shames that you have stained me with,
Supply your present wants, and take no doit
Of usance for my moneys, and you'll not hear me:
This is kind I offer.
  Antonio. This were kindness!
  Shylock.   This kindness will I show. 140
Go with me to a notary, seal me there
Your single bond, and, in a merry sport,
If you repay me not on such a day,
In such a place, such sum or sums as are
Expressed in the condition, let the forfeit
Be nominated for an equal pound
Of your fair flesh, to be cut off and taken
In what part of your body pleaseth me.
  Antonio. Content, in faith—I'll seal to such a bond,
And say there is much kindness in the Jew.   150
  Bassanio. You shall not seal to such a bond for me,
I'll rather dwell in my necessity.
  Antonio. Why, fear not man, I will not forfeit it.
Within these two months, that's a month before
This bond expires, I do expect return
Of thrice three times the value of this bond.

Shylock. O father Abram! what these Christians are,
Whose own hard dealing teaches them suspect
The thoughts of others. Pray you, tell me this—
160 If he should break his day, what should I gain
By the exaction of the forfeiture?
A pound of man's flesh, taken from a man,
Is not so estimable, profitable neither,
As flesh of muttons, beefs, or goats. I say,
To buy his favour, I extend this friendship.
If he will take it, so—if not, adieu,
And, for my love, I pray you wrong me not.
   Antonio. Yes, Shylock, I will seal unto this bond.
   Shylock. Then meet me forthwith at the notary's,
170 Give him direction for this merry bond,
And I will go and purse the ducats straight,
See to my house left in the fearful guard
Of an unthrifty knave; and presently
I will be with you.
   Antonio.   Hie thee, gentle Jew....

                         [Shylock enters his house
The Hebrew will turn Christian—he grows kind.
   Bassanio. I like not fair terms and a villain's mind.
   Antonio. Come on—in this there can be no dismay,
My ships come home a month before the day.

                               [they walk away

[2.1.]   *The hall of Portia's house at Belmont*

Enter the Prince of MOROCCO, *'a tawny Moor all in white, and three or four followers accordingly, with* PORTIA, NERISSA, *and their train'*

   Morocco. Mislike me not for my complexion,
The shadowed livery of the burnished sun,
To whom I am a neighbour and near bred.

Bring me the fairest creature northward born,
Where Phœbus' fire scarce thaws the icicles,
And let us make incision for your love,
To prove whose blood is reddest, his or mine.
I tell thee, lady, this aspéct of mine
Hath feared the valiant. By my love, I swear
The best-regarded virgins of our clime 10
Have loved it too. I would not change this hue,
Except to steal your thoughts, my gentle queen.
  Portia. In terms of choice I am not solely led
By nice direction of a maiden's eyes:
Besides, the lott'ry of my destiny
Bars me the right of voluntary choosing:
But if my father had not scanted me
And hedged me by his wit, to yield myself
His wife who wins me by that means I told you,
Yourself, renownéd prince, then stood as fair 20
As any comer I have looked on yet
For my affection.
  Morocco.   Even for that I thank you.
Therefore, I pray you, lead me to the caskets
To try my fortune. By this scimitar—
That slew the Sophy and a Persian prince
That won three fields of Sultan Solyman—
I would o'erstare the sternest eyes that look:
Outbrave the heart most daring on the earth:
Pluck the young sucking cubs from the she-bear,
Yea, mock the lion when a' roars for prey, 30
To win thee, lady. But alas the while!
If Hercules and Lichas play at dice
Which is the better man, the greater throw
May turn by fortune from the weaker hand:
So is Alcides, beaten by his page,
And so may I, blind fortune leading me,

Miss that which one unworthier may attain,
And die with grieving.

    Portia.   You must take your chance—
And either not attempt to choose at all,
40 Or swear, before you choose, if you choose wrong,
Never to speak to lady afterward
In way of marriage. Therefore be advised.

    Morocco. Nor will not. Come, bring me unto my chance.

    Portia. First, forward to the temple. After dinner
Your hazard shall be made.

    Morocco.   Good fortune then!
To make me blest or cursed'st among men.   *[they go*

[2.2.]   *The street before Shylock's house*

    LANCELOT GOBBO *comes forth, scratching his head*

    Lancelot. Certainly my conscience will serve me to
run from this Jew my master. The fiend is at mine
elbow, and tempts me, saying to me, 'Gobbo, Lancelot
Gobbo, good Lancelot,' or 'good Gobbo,' or 'good
Lancelot Gobbo, use your legs, take the start, run
away.' My conscience says, 'No; take heed honest
Lancelot, take heed honest Gobbo,' or as aforesaid,
'honest Lancelot Gobbo, do not run, scorn running
with thy heels'. Well, the most courageous fiend bids
10 me pack. 'Fia!' says the fiend, 'away!' says the fiend,
'for the heavens, rouse up a brave mind,' says the fiend,
'and run'. Well, my conscience, hanging about the
neck of my heart, says very wisely to me: 'My honest
friend, Lancelot, being an honest man's son,'—or rather
an honest woman's son—for indeed my father did something smack, something grow to; he had a kind of
taste; well, my conscience says, 'Lancelot, budge not.'
'Budge,' says the fiend. 'Budge not,' says my con-

science. 'Conscience,' say I, 'you counsel well.' '
'Fiend,' say I, 'you counsel well.' To be ruled by my 20
conscience, I should stay with the Jew my master, who
(God bless the mark!) is a kind of devil; and to run
away from the Jew, I should be ruled by the fiend, who,
saving your reverence, is the devil himself. Certainly,
the Jew is the very devil incarnation—and, in my conscience, my conscience is but a kind of hard conscience,
to offer to counsel me to stay with the Jew. The fiend
gives the more friendly counsel. I will run, fiend. My
heels are at your commandment, I will run.

He runs, and stumbles into the arms of Old GOBBO,
who comes along the street '*with a basket*'

Old Gobbo [*gasps*]. Master young-man, you I pray 30
you, which is the way to Master Jew's?
Lancelot. O heavens, this is my true-begotten father,
who being more than sand-blind, high gravel-blind,
knows me not. I will try confusions with him.
Old Gobbo. Master, young gentleman, I pray· you
which is the way to Master Jew's?
Lancelot [*shouts in his ear*]. Turn up on your right
hand at the next turning, but at the next turning of all
on your left; marry at the very next turning turn of no
hand, but turn down indirectly to the Jew's house. 40
Old Gobbo. Be God's sonties, 'twill be a hard way to
hit. Can you tell me whether one Lancelot that dwells
with him, dwell with him or no?
Lancelot. Talk you of young Master Lancelot?—
[*aside*] Mark me now, now will I raise the waters!
Talk you of young Master Lancelot?
Old Gobbo. No 'master,' sir, but a poor man's son.
His father, though I say't, is an honest exceeding poor
man, and God be thanked well to live.

50 *Lancelot.* Well, let his father be what a' will, we
talk of young Master Lancelot.

Old Gobbo. Your worship's friend and Lancelot, sir.

Lancelot. But I pray you ergo old man, ergo I
beseech you, talk you of young Master Lancelot.

Old Gobbo. Of Lancelot, an't please your mastership.

Lancelot. Ergo—Master Lancelot! Talk not of
Master Lancelot, father, for the young gentleman—
according to fates and destinies, and such odd sayings,
the sisters three, and such branches of learning—is indeed
60 deceased, or as you would say in plain terms, gone to
heaven.

Old Gobbo. Marry, God forbid! the boy was the very
staff of my age, my very prop.

Lancelot. Do I look like a cudgel or a hovel-post,
a staff or a prop?
Do you know me, father?

Old Gobbo. Alack the day, I know you not, young
gentleman, but I pray you tell me, is my boy—God rest
his soul!—alive or dead?

70 *Lancelot.* Do you not know me, father?

Old Gobbo. Alack, sir, I am sand-blind, I know you not.

Lancelot. Nay, indeed, if you had your eyes, you
might fail of the knowing me: it is a wise father that
knows his own child. [*he kneels*] Well, old man, I
will tell you news of your son. Give me your blessing.
Truth will come to light, murder cannot be hid long,
a man's son may, but in the end truth will out.

Old Gobbo. Pray you, sir, stand up. I am sure you are
not Lancelot, my boy.

80 *Lancelot.* Pray you let's have no more fooling about
it, but give me your blessing: I am Lancelot, your
boy that was, your son that is, your child that shall be.

Old Gobbo. I cannot think you are my son.

Lancelot. I know not what I shall think of that: but I am Lancelot, the Jew's man, and I am sure Margery, your wife, is my mother.

Old Gobbo. Her name is Margery, indeed. I'll be sworn, if thou be Lancelot, thou art mine own flesh and blood...[*he feels for Lancelot's face; Lancelot bows and presents the nape of his neck*] Lord worshipped might 90 he be! what a beard hast thou got! thou hast got more hair on thy chin than Dobbin my fill-horse has on his tail.

Lancelot. It should seem then that Dobbin's tail grows backward. I am sure he had more hair of his tail than I have of my face, when I last saw him.

Old Gobbo. Lord, how art thou changed! How dost thou and thy master agree? I have brought him a present. How 'gree you now?

Lancelot. Well, well—but, for mine own part, as I have set up my rest to run away, so I will not rest till 100 I have run some ground. My master's a very Jew— give him a present! give him a halter—I am famished in his service: you may tell every finger I have with my ribs. Father, I am glad you are come. Give me your present to one Master Bassanio, who indeed gives rare new liveries. If I serve not him, I will run as far as God has any ground. O rare fortune! here comes the man—to him, father, for I am a Jew if I serve the Jew any longer.

BASSANIO *approaches with* LEONARDO *and other followers*

Bassanio [*talking to a servant*]. You may do so, but let 110 it be so hasted that supper be ready at the farthest by five of the clock. See these letters delivered, put the liveries to making, and desire Gratiano to come anon to my lodging.   [*the servant goes*

Lancelot [*thrusting forward the old man*]. To him, father.

Old Gobbo [*bows*]. God bless your worship!

Bassanio. Gramercy, wouldst thou aught with me?

Old Gobbo. Here's my son, sir, a poor boy—

120 *Lancelot* [*comes forward himself*]. Not a poor boy, sir, but the rich Jew's man that would, sir, as my father shall specify— [*retreats behind his father*

Old Gobbo. He hath a great infection, sir, as one would say to serve—

Lancelot [*comes forward*]. Indeed the short and the long is, I serve the Jew, and have a desire as my father shall specify— [*retreats*

Old Gobbo. His master and he (saving your worship's reverence) are scarce cater-cousins—

130 *Lancelot* [*comes forward*]. To be brief, the very truth is, that the Jew having done me wrong, doth cause me as my father being I hope an old man shall frutify unto you— [*retreats*

Old Gobbo. I have here a dish of doves that I would bestow upon your worship, and my suit is—

Lancelot [*comes forward*]. In very brief, the suit is impertinent to myself, as your worship shall know by this honest old man, and though I say it, though old man, yet poor man, my father.

140 *Bassanio.* One speak for both. What would you?

Lancelot. Serve you, sir.

Old Gobbo. That is the very defect of the matter, sir.

Bassanio. I know thee well, thou hast obtained thy suit.
Shylock, thy master, spoke with me this day,
And hath preferred thee, if it be preferment
To leave a rich Jew's service, to become
The follower of so poor a gentleman.

Lancelot. The old proverb is very well parted

between my master Shylock and you, sir—you have
'the grace of God,' sir, and he hath 'enough.'   150
 Bassanio. Thou speak'st it well; go, father, with
  thy son.
Take leave of thy old master, and inquire
My lodging out. [*to his followers*] Give him a livery
More guarded than his fellows': see it done.
      [*he talks with Leonardo apart*
 Lancelot. Father, in. I cannot get a service, no!
I have ne'er a tongue in my head! Well...[*looking on his
palm*] if any man in Italy have a fairer table which doth
offer to swear upon a book I shall have good fortune.
Go to, here's a simple line of life, here's a small trifle
of wives—alas, fifteen wives is nothing, eleven widows, 160
and nine maids, is a simple coming-in for one man—
and then to scape drowning thrice, and to be in peril
of my life with the edge of a feather-bed. Here are simple
scapes. Well, if Fortune be a woman, she's a good
wench for this gear. Father, come. I'll take my leave
of the Jew in the twinkling.
   [*Lancelot and Old Gobbo enter Shylock's house*
 Bassanio. I pray thee, good Leonardo, think on this.
These things being bought and orderly bestowed,
Return in haste, for I do feast to-night
My best-esteemed acquaintance. Hie thee, go.   170
 Leonardo. My best endeavours shall be done herein.

   As he goes off he meets GRATIANO
    coming along the street

 Gratiano. Where's your master?
 Leonardo.   Yonder, sir, he walks.
         [*Leonardo departs*
 Gratiano. Signior Bassanio!
 Bassanio.   Gratiano!

Gratiano. I have a suit to you.

Bassanio. You have obtained it.

Gratiano. You must not deny me—I must go with you to Belmont.

Bassanio. Why, then you must. But hear thee Gratiano,
Thou art too wild, too rude, and bold of voice—
Parts that become thee happily enough,
180 And in such eyes as ours appear not faults;
But where thou art not known, why, there they show
Something too liberal. Pray thee, take pain
To allay with some cold drops of modesty
Thy skipping spirit, lest through thy wild behaviour
I be misćonstrued in the place I go to,
And lose my hopes.

Gratiano. Signior Bassanio, hear me—
If I do not put on a sober habit,
Talk with respect, and swear but now and then,
Wear prayer-books in my pocket, look demurely,
190 Nay more, while grace is saying, hood mine eyes
Thus with my hat, and sigh, and say 'amen';
Use all the observance of civility,
Like one well studied in a sad ostent
To please his grandam, never trust me more.

Bassanio. Well, we shall see your bearing.

Gratiano. Nay, but I bar to-night, you shall not gauge me
By what we do to-night.

Bassanio. No, that were pity,
I would entreat you rather to put on
Your boldest suit of mirth, for we have friends
200 That purpose merriment. But fare you well,
I have some business.

Gratiano. And I must to Lorenzo, and the rest.
But we will visit you at supper-time.

[*they go their way*

[2.3.] *The door opens: JESSICA and LANCELOT come forth*

Jessica. I am sorry thou wilt leave my father so—
Our house is hell, and thou, a merry devil,
Didst rob it of some taste of tediousness.
But fare thee well, there is a ducat for thee.
And, Lancelot, soon at supper shalt thou see
Lorenzo, who is thy new master's guest,
Give him this letter, do it secretly,
And so farewell: I would not have my father
See me in talk with thee.

Lancelot. Adieu! tears exhibit my tongue. Most 10
beautiful pagan, most sweet Jew! if a Christian do not
play the knave and get thee, I am much deceived. But
adieu, these foolish drops do something drown my
manly spirit; adieu!   [*he goes*

Jessica. Farewell, good Lancelot.
Alack, what heinous sin is it in me
To be ashamed to be my father's child!
But though I am a daughter to his blood,
I am not to his manners. O Lorenzo,
If thou keep promise, I shall end this strife,   20
Become a Christian, and thy loving wife. [*she goes within*

[2.4.]   *Another street in Venice*

   GRATIANO, LORENZO, SALERIO and SOLANIO
           in lively conversation

Lorenzo. Nay, we will slink away in supper-time,
Disguise us at my lodging, and return
All in an hour.

Gratiano. We have not made good preparation.

Salerio. We have not spoke as yet of torch-bearers.

Solanio. 'Tis vile, unless it may be quaintly ordered,
And better in my mind not undertook.

Lorenzo. 'Tis now but four o'clock—we have two hours
To furnish us.   LANCELOT *comes up*

               Friend Lancelot, what's the news?

10 *Lancelot* [*takes a letter from his wallet*]. An it shall
please you to break up this, it shall seem to signify.

    Lorenzo. I know the hand. In faith 'tis a fair hand,
And whiter than the paper it writ on,
Is the fair hand that writ.

    Gratiano.   Love-news, in faith.

    Lancelot. By your leave, sir.

    Lorenzo. Whither goest thou?

    Lancelot. Marry, sir, to bid my old master the Jew
to sup to-night with my new master the Christian.

    Lorenzo. Hold here, take this.   [*he gives him money*
                      'Tell gentle Jessica
20 I will not fail her—speak it privately.   [*Lancelot goes*
Go, gentlemen,
Will you prepare you for this masque to-night?
I am provided of a torch-bearer.

    Salerio. Ay, marry, I'll be gone about it straight.

    Solanio. And so will I.

    Lorenzo.   Meet me and Gratiano
At Gratiano's lodging some hour hence.

    Salerio. 'Tis good we do so.

                 [*Salerio and Solanio leave them*

    Gratiano. Was not that letter from fair Jessica?

    Lorenzo. I must needs tell thee all. She hath directed
30 How I shall take her from her father's house,
What gold and jewels she is furnished with,
What page's suit she hath in readiness.
If e'er the Jew her father come to heaven
It will be for his gentle daughter's sake,
And never dare misfortune cross her foot

Unless she do it under this excuse—
That she is issue to a faithless Jew.
Come, go with me. Peruse this, as thou goest.
Fair Jessica shall be my torch-bearer.   [*they walk on*

[2.5.]   *The street before Shylock's house*

SHYLOCK *and* LANCELOT *come forth*

Shylock. Well, thou shalt see, thy eyes shall be
    thy judge,
The difference of old Shylock and Bassanio—
What, Jessica!—Thou shalt not gormandise,
As thou hast done with me—What, Jessica!—
And sleep and snore, and rend apparel out—
Why, Jessica, I say!
Lancelot [*bawls*].   Why, Jessica!
Shylock. Who bids thee call? I do not bid thee call.
Lancelot. Your worship was wont to tell me I could
do nothing without bidding.

JESSICA appears at the door

Jessica. Call you? What is your will?   10
Shylock. I am bid forth to supper, Jessica.
There are my keys...But wherefore should I go?
I am not bid for love—they flatter me.
But yet I'll go in hate, to feed upon
The prodigal Christian. Jessica, my girl,
Look to my house. I am right loath to go:
There is some ill a-brewing towards my rest,
For I did dream of money-bags to-night.
Lancelot. I beseech you, sir, go. My young master
doth expect your reproach.   20
Shylock. So do I his.
Lancelot. And they have conspired together—I will

not say you shall see a masque, but if you do, then it
was not for nothing that my nose fell a-bleeding on
Black-Monday last, at six o'clock i'th' morning, falling
out that year on Ash-Wednesday was four year, in
th'afternoon.

   Shylock. What, are there masques? Hear you me,
       Jessica—
Lock up my doors, and when you hear the drum
30 And the vile squealing of the wry-necked fife,
Clamber not you up to the casements then,
Nor thrust your head into the public street
To gaze on Christian fools with varnished faces:
But stop my house's ears, I mean my casements,
Let not the sound of shallow fopp'ry enter
My sober house. By Jacob's staff I swear
I have no mind of feasting forth to-night:
But I will go. Go you before me, sirrah—
Say I will come.

   Lancelot.   I will go before, sir....
        [as he departs he passes by the door and whispers
40 Mistress, look out at window, for all this—
        There will come a Christian by,
        Will be worth a Jewess' eye.   *[he goes*
   Shylock. What says that fool of Hagar's offspring, ha?
   Jessica. His words were, 'Farewell, mistress'—
nothing else.
   Shylock. The patch is kind enough, but a huge feeder,
Snail-slow in profit, and he sleeps by day
More than the wild-cat: drones hive not with me.
Therefore I part with him, and part with him
To one that I would have him help to waste
50 His borrowed purse. Well, Jessica, go in.
Perhaps I will return immediately.
Do as I bid you, shut doors after you.

Fast bind, fast find,
A proverb never stale in thrifty mind.   [*he goes*

   Jessica. Farewell—and if my fortune be not crost,
I have a father, you a daughter, lost.   [*she goes within*

[2.6.]   *GRATIANO and SALERIO come up,*
        in masquing attire

   Gratiano. This is the pent-house, under which Lorenzo
Desired us to make stand.
   Salerio.   His hour is almost past.
   Gratiano. And it is marvel he out-dwells his hour,
For lovers ever run before the clock.
   Salerio. O, ten times faster Venus' pigeons fly
To seal love's bonds new-made, than they are wont
To keep obligéd faith unforfeited!
   Gratiano. That ever holds: who riseth from a feast
With that keen appetite that he sits down?
Where is the horse that doth untread again   10
His tedious measures with the unbated fire
That he did pace them first? All things that are,
Are with more spirit chaséd than enjoyed.
How like a younger or a prodigal
The scarféd bark puts from her native bay,
Hugged and embracéd by the strumpet wind!
How like the prodigal doth she return,
With over-weathered ribs and ragged sails,
Lean, rent and beggared by the strumpet wind!

      LORENZO approaches in haste

   Salerio. Here comes Lorenzo—more of this hereafter. 20
   Lorenzo. Sweet friends, your patience for my
     long abode.
Not I, but my affairs, have made you wait:
When you shall please to play the thieves for wives

I'll watch as long for you then. Approach.
Here dwells my father Jew. Ho! who's within?

A casement window opens above the door
and JESSICA leans out, clad as a boy

Jessica. Who are you? Tell me, for more certainty,
Albeit I'll swear that I do know your tongue.
    Lorenzo. Lorenzo, and thy love.
    Jessica. Lorenzo, certain, and my love indeed,
30 For who love I so much? And now who knows
But you, Lorenzo, whether I am yours?
    Lorenzo. Heaven and thy thoughts are witness
      that thou art.
    Jessica. Here, catch this casket, it is worth the pains.
                           [she casts it down
I am glad 'tis night, you do not look on me,
For I am much ashamed of my exchange:
But love is blind, and lovers cannot see
The pretty follies that themselves commit,
For if they could, Cupid himself would blush
To see me thus transforméd to a boy.
40   *Lorenzo.* Descend, for you must be my torch-bearer.
    Jessica. What, must I hold a candle to my shames?
They in themselves, good sooth, are too too light.
Why, 'tis an office of discovery, love,
And I should be obscured.
    Lorenzo.   So are you, sweet,
Even in the lovely garnish of a boy.
But come at once,
For the close night doth play the runaway,
And we are stayed for at Bassanio's feast.
    Jessica. I will make fast the doors, and gild myself
50 With some moe ducats, and be with you straight.
                       [she closes the casement
    Gratiano. Now, by my hood, a gentle and no Jew.

Lorenzo. Beshrew me but I love her heartily,
For she is wise, if I can judge of her,
And fair she is, if that mine eyes be true,
And true she is, as she hath proved herself:
And therefore, like herself, wise, fair, and true,
Shall she be placéd in my constant soul.

         JESSICA comes from the house

What, art thou come? On, gentlemen, away—
Our masquing mates by this time for us stay.

         [he departs with Jessica and Salerio

         ANTONIO comes along the street·

Antonio. Who's there?   60
Gratiano. Signior Antonio?
Antonio. Fie, fie, Gratiano! where are all the rest?
'Tis nine o'clock—our friends all stay for you.
No masque to-night, the wind is come about,
Bassanio presently will go aboard.
I have sent twenty out to seek for you.
Gratiano. I am glad on't. I desire no more delight
Than to be under sail and gone to-night.   *[they go*

[2.7.] *The hall of Portia's house at Belmont; PORTIA
enters, with the Prince of MOROCCO, and their trains*

Portia. Go, draw aside the curtains, and discover
The several caskets to this noble prince.

    *Servants draw back the curtains and reveal a table
         and three caskets thereon*

Now make your choice. *[Morocco examines the caskets*
Morocco. The first, of gold, who this inscription bears:
'Who chooseth me shall gain what many men desire'.
The second, silver, which this promise carries:
'Who chooseth me shall get as much as he deserves'.

This third, dull lead, with warning all as blunt:
'Who chooseth me must give and hazard all he hath'.
10 How shall I know if I do choose the right?

   Portia. The one of them contains my picture, prince.
If you choose that, then I am yours withal.

   Morocco. Some god direct my judgement! Let me see,
I will survey th'inscriptions back again.
What says this leaden casket?
'Who chooseth me must give and hazard all he hath.'
Must give—for what? for lead? hazard for lead?
This casket threatens. Men that hazard all
Do it in hope of fair advantages:
20 A golden mind stoops not to shows of dross.
I'll then nor give nor hazard aught for lead.
What says the silver with her virgin hue?
'Who chooseth me shall get as much as he deserves.'
As much as he deserves! Pause there, Morocco,
And weigh thy value with an even hand.
If thou be'st rated by thy estimation,
Thou dost deserve enough—and yet enough
May not extend so far as to the lady:
And yet to be afeard of my deserving
30 Were but a weak disabling of myself.
As much as I deserve! Why, that's the lady.
I do in birth deserve her, and in fortunes,
In graces, and in qualities of breeding:
But more than these, in love I do deserve.
What if I strayed no further, but chose here?
Let's see once more this saying graved in gold:
'Who chooseth me shall gain what many men desire'.
Why, that's the lady—all the world desires her.
From the four corners of the earth they come,
40 To kiss this shrine, this mortal-breathing saint.
The Hyrcanian deserts and the vasty wilds

Of wide Arabia are as throughfares now
For princes to come view fair Portia.
The watery kingdom, whose ambitious head
Spets in the face of heaven, is no bar
To stop the foreign spirits, but they come,
As o'er a brook, to see fair Portia.
One of these three contains her heavenly picture.
Is't like that lead contains her? 'Twere damnation
To think so base a thought—it were too gross   50
To rib her cerecloth in the obscure grave.
Or shall I think in silver she's immured,
Being ten times undervalued to tried gold?
O sinful thought! Never so rich a gem
Was set in worse than gold.   They have in England
A coin that bears the figure of an angel
Stampéd in gold, but that's insculped upon;
But here an angel in a golden bed
Lies all within....Deliver me the key:
Here do I choose, and thrive I as I may!   60
  Portia. There, take it, prince, and if my form
        lie there,
Then I am yours.   [*he unlocks the golden casket*
  Morocco.   O hell! what have we here?
A carrion Death, within whose empty eye
There is a written scroll! I'll read the writing.
        'All that glisters is not gold,
          Often have you heard that told.
          Many a man his life hath sold,
          But my outside to behold.
          Gilded tombs do worms infold.
          Had you been as wise as bold,   70
          Young in limbs, in judgement old,
          Your answer had not been inscrolled—
          Fare you well, your suit is cold.'

Cold, indeed, and labour lost.
Then, farewell heat, and welcome frost.
Portia, adieu! I have too grieved a heart
To take a tedious leave: thus losers part.

                    [*he departs with his retinue*

 Portia. A gentle riddance. Draw the curtains, go.
Let all of his complexion choose me so. [*they go out*

[2.8.]   *A street in Venice*

SALERIO *and* SOLANIO

 Salerio. Why man, I saw Bassanio under sail,
With him is Gratiano gone along;
And in their ship I am sure Lorenzo is not.
 Solanio. The villain Jew with outcries raised the duke,
Who went with him to search Bassanio's ship.
 Salerio. He came too late, the ship was under sail,
But there the duke was given to understand
That in a gondola were seen together
Lorenzo and his amorous Jessica.
10 Besides, Antonio certified the duke
They were not with Bassanio in his ship.
 Solanio. I never heard a passion so confused,
So strange, outrageous, and so variable,
As the dog Jew did utter in the streets.
'My daughter! O my ducats! O my daughter!
Fled with a Christian! O my Christian ducats!
Justice! the law! my ducats, and my daughter!
A sealéd bag, two sealéd bags of ducats,
Of double ducats, stol'n from me by my daughter!
20 And jewels—two stones, two rich and precious stones,
Stol'n by my daughter! Justice! find the girl!
She hath the stones upon her, and the ducats!'

Salerio. Why, all the boys in Venice follow him,
Crying, his stones, his daughter, and his ducats.
Solanio. Let good Antonio look he keep his day,
Or he shall pay for this.
Salerio.   Marry, well remembred:
I reasoned with a Frenchman yesterday,
Who told me, in the narrow seas that part
The French and English, there miscarriéd
A vessel of our country richly fraught: 30
I thought upon Antonio when he told me,
And wished in silence that it were not his.
Solanio. You were best to tell Antonio what you hear—
Yet do not suddenly, for it may grieve him.
Salerio. A kinder gentleman treads not the earth.
I saw Bassanio and Antonio part.
Bassanio told him he would make some speed
Of his return: he answered, 'Do not so.
Slubber not business for my sake, Bassanio,
But stay the very riping of the time.   40
And for the Jew's bond which he hath of me,
Let it not enter in your mind of love:
Be merry, and employ your chiefest thoughts
To courtship, and such fair ostents of love
As shall conveniently become you there.'
And even there, his eye being big with tears,
Turning his face, he put his hand behind him,
And with affection wondrous sensible
He wrung Bassanio's hand, and so they parted.
Solanio. I think he only loves the world for him.   50
I pray thee, let us go and find him out,
And quicken his embracéd heaviness
With some delight or other.
Salerio.   Do we so.   [*they pass on*

[2.9.]   *The hall of Portia's house at Belmont*

A servitor on guard before the curtains;
NERISSA enters in haste

Nerissa. Quick, quick, I pray thee—draw the
     curtain straight.
The Prince of Arragon hath ta'en his oath,
And comes to his election presently.
                              [*the curtains are drawn aside*

PORTIA enters with the Prince of ARRAGON,
and their trains

Portia. Behold, there stand the caskets, noble prince.
If you choose that wherein I am contained,
Straight shall our nuptial rites be solemnized:
But if you fail, without more speech, my lord,
You must be gone from hence immediately.
     Arragon. I am enjoined by oath to observe
          three things—
10 First, never to unfold to any one
Which casket 'twas I chose; next, if I fail
Of the right casket, never in my life
To woo a maid in way of marriage;
Lastly,
If I do fail in fortune of my choice,
Immediately to leave you and be gone.
     Portia. To these injunctions every one doth swear,
That comes to hazard for my worthless self.
     Arragon. And so have I addressed me. Fortune now
20 To my heart's hope!   [*he turns to look upon the caskets*
                         Gold, silver, and base lead.
'Who chooseth me must give and hazard all he hath '
You shall look fairer, ere I give or hazard.

What says the golden chest? ha! let me see:
'Who chooseth me shall gain what many men desire.'
What many men desire! that 'many' may be meant
By the fool multitude, that choose by show,
Not learning more than the fond eye doth teach;
Which pries not to th'interior, but like the martlet,
Builds in the weather on the outward wall,
Even in the force and road of casualty.   30
I will not choose what many men desire,
Because I will not jump with common spirits,
And rank me with the barbarous multitudes.
Why, then to thee, thou silver treasure-house!
Tell me once more what title thou dost bear:
'Who chooseth me shall get as much as he deserves.'
And well said too; for who shall go about
To cozen fortune and be honourable
Without the stamp of merit. Let none presume
To wear an undeservéd dignity.   40
O, that estates, degrees and offices,
Were not derived corruptly, and that clear honour
Were purchased by the merit of the wearer—
How many then should cover that stand bare!
How many be commanded that command!
How much low peasantry would then be gleaned
From the true seed of honour! and how much honour
Picked from the chaff and ruin of the times,
To be new varnished! Well, but to my choice.
'Who chooseth me shall get as much as he deserves.'   50
I will assume desert. [*he takes up the silver casket*] Give
    me a key for this—
And instantly unlock my fortunes here.
            [*he opens the casket, and starts back amazed*
(*Portia.* Too long a pause for that which you
    find there.

Arragon. What's here? the portrait of a blinking idiot,
Presenting me a schedule! I will read it.
How much unlike art thou to Portia!
How much unlike my hopes and my deservings!
'Who chooseth me shall have as much as he deserves.'
Did I deserve no more than a fool's head?
60 Is that my prize? are my deserts no better?

Portia. To offend and judge are distinct offices,
And of oppos'd natures.

Arragon [*unfolds the paper*].   What is here?

    'The fire seven times tried this—
    Seven times tried that judgement is,
    That did never choose amiss.
    Some there be that shadows kiss,
    Such have but a shadow's bliss:
    There be fools alive, I wis,
    Silvered o'er—and so was this.
70   Take what wife you will to bed,
    I will ever be your head:
    So be gone, you are sped.'

    Still more fool I shall appear
    By the time I linger here.
    With one fool's head I came to woo,
    But I go away with two.
    Sweet, adieu! I'll keep my oath,
    Patiently to bear my roth.

                [*he departs with his train*

Portia. Thus hath the candle singed the moth:
80 O, these deliberate fools! when they do choose,
They have the wisdom by their wit to lose.

Nerissa. The ancient saying is no heresy,
Hanging and wiving goes by destiny.

Portia. Come, draw the curtain, Nerissa. [*she does so*

A servant enters

Servant. Where is my lady?

Portia.   Here—what would my lord?

Servant. Madam, there is alighted at your gate
A young Venetian, one that comes before
To signify th'approaching of his lord,
From whom he bringeth sensible regreets:
To wit, besides commends and courteous breath,   90
Gifts of rich value...Yet I have not seen
So likely an ambassador of love.
A day in April never came so sweet,
To show how costly summer was at hand,
As this fore-spurrer comes before his lord.

Portia. No more, I pray thee. I am half afeard,
Thou wilt say anon he is some kin to thee,
Thou spend'st such high-day wit in praising him.
Come, come, Nerissa, for I long to see
Quick Cupid's post that comes so mannerly.   100

Nerissa. Bassanio—Lord Love, if thy will it be! [*they go*

[3.1.]   *The street before Shylock's house*

SOLANIO *and* SALERIO *meeting*

Solanio. Now, what news on the Rialto?

Salerio. Why, yet it lives there unchecked that
Antonio hath a ship of rich lading wracked on the
narrow seas; the Goodwins, I think they call the place—
a very dangerous flat and fatal, where the carcases of
many a tall ship lie buried, as they say, if my gossip
Report be an honest woman of her word.

Solanio. I would she were as lying a gossip in that,
as ever knapped ginger, or made her neighbours believe
she wept for the death of a third husband. But it is   10

true, without any slips of prolixity or crossing the plain highway of talk, that the good Antonio, the honest Antonio—O, that I had a title good enough to keep his name company—

Salerio. Come, the full stop.

Solanio. Ha! what sayest thou? Why, the end is, he hath lost a ship.

Salerio. I would it might prove the end of his losses.

Solanio. Let me say 'amen' betimes, lest the devil
20 cross my prayer, for here he comes in the likeness of a Jew....

SHYLOCK *comes from his house*

How now, Shylock! what news among the merchants?

Shylock [*turns upon them*]. You knew, none so well, none so well as you, of my daughter's flight.

Salerio. That's certain! I, for my part, knew the tailor that made the wings she flew withal.

Solanio. And Shylock, for his own part, knew the bird was fledge, and then it is the complexion of them all to leave the dam.

30 *Shylock.* She is damned for it.

Salerio. That's certain, if the devil may be her judge.

Shylock. My own flesh and blood to rebel!

Solanio. Out upon it, old carrion, rebels it at these years?

Shylock. I say, my daughter is my flesh and blood.

Salerio. There is more difference between thy flesh and hers than between jet and ivory, more between your bloods than there is between red wine and rhenish. But tell us, do you hear whether Antonio have had any
40 loss at sea or no?

Shylock. There I have another bad match—a bankrupt, a prodigal, who dare scarce show his head on the

Rialto, a beggar that was used to come so smug upon the mart. Let him look to his bond! he was wont to call me usurer, let him look to his bond! he was wont to lend money for a Christian curtsy, let him look to his bond!

Salerio. Why, I am sure, if he forfeit, thou wilt not take his flesh—what's that good for?

Shylock. To bait fish withal! if it will feed nothing else, it will feed my revenge. He hath disgraced me and 50 hindred me half a million, laughed at my losses, mocked at my gains, scorned my nation, thwarted my bargains, cooled my friends, heated mine enemies—and what's his reason? I am a Jew. Hath not a Jew eyes? hath not a Jew hands, organs, dimensions, senses, affections, passions? fed with the same food, hurt with the same weapons, subject to the same diseases, healed by the same means, warmed and cooled by the same winter and summer, as a Christian is? If you prick us, do we not bleed? if you tickle us, do we not laugh? if you 60 poison us, do we not die? and if you wrong us, shall we not revenge? if we are like you in the rest, we will resemble you in that. If a Jew wrong a Christian, what is his humility? Revenge. If a Christian wrong a Jew, what should his sufferance be by Christian example? Why, revenge. The villainy you teach me I will execute, and it shall go hard but I will better the instruction.

A servant accosts Solanio and Salerio

Servant. Gentlemen, my master Antonio is at his house, and desires to speak with you both.

Salerio. We have been up and down to seek him. 70

TUBAL appears making for Shylock's house

Solanio. Here comes another of the tribe—a third cannot be matched, unless the devil himself turn Jew.

[*Solanio and Salerio depart, followed by the servant*

Shylock. How now, Tubal! what news from Genoa? hast thou found my daughter?

Tubal. I often came where I did hear of her, but cannot find her.

Shylock. Why there, there, there, there—a diamond gone, cost me two thousand ducats in Frankfort—the curse never fell upon our nation till now, I never felt it
80 till now—two thousand ducats in that, and other precious, precious jewels. I would my daughter were dead at my foot, and the jewels in her ear! would she were hearsed at my foot, and the ducats in her coffin! No news of them? Why, so—and I know not what's spent in the search: why, thou loss upon loss! the thief gone with so much and so much to find the thief, and no satisfaction, no revenge, nor no ill luck stirring but what lights o' my shoulders, no sighs but o' my breathing, no tears but o' my shedding. [*he weeps*
90 *Tubal.* Yes, other men have ill luck too. Antonio, as I heard in Genoa—

Shylock. What, what, what? ill luck, ill luck?

Tubal. —hath an argosy cast away, coming from Tripolis.

Shylock. I thank God, I thank God! Is it true? is it true?

Tubal. I spoke with some of the sailors that escaped the wrack.

Shylock. I thank thee good Tubal, good news, good
100 news: ha, ha! Heard in Genoa?

Tubal. Your daughter spent in Genoa, as I heard, one night, fourscore ducats.

Shylock. Thou stick'st a dagger in me. I shall never see my gold again—fourscore ducats at a sitting! fourscore ducats!

Tubal. There came divers of Antonio's creditors in

my company to Venice, that swear he cannot choose
but break.

Shylock. I am very glad of it, I'll plague him, I'll
torture him, I am glad of it.   110

Tubal. One of them showed me a ring that he had
of your daughter for a monkey.

Shylock. Out upon her! thou torturest me, Tubal—it was
my turquoise—I had it of Leah when I was a bachelor:
I would not have given it for a wilderness of monkeys.

Tubal. But Antonio is certainly undone.

Shylock. Nay, that's true, that's very true, go Tubal,
fee me an officer, bespeak him a fortnight before. I will
have the heart of him if he forfeit, for were he out of
Venice I can make what merchandise I will. Go, 120
Tubal, and meet me at our synagogue—go, good Tubal
—at our synagogue, Tubal.

              [Tubal departs and Shylock goes within

[3.2.] *The hall of Portia's house at Belmont; the curtains
are drawn back from before the caskets; in the gallery
sit musicians*

BASSANIO *with* PORTIA, GRATIANO *with* NERISSA;
the servitor and other attendants

Portia. I pray you tarry, pause a day or two
Before you hazard, for in choosing wrong
I lose your company; therefore, forbear awhile.
There's something tells me (but it is not love)
I would not lose you, and you know yourself,
Hate counsels not in such a quality;
But lest you should not understand me well—
And yet a maiden hath no tongue but thought—
I would detain you here some month or two
Before you venture for me.   I could teach you   10

How to choose right, but then I am forsworn,
So will I never be, so may you miss me;
But if you do, you'll make me wish a sin,
That I had been forsworn. Beshrew your eyes,
They have o'er-looked me and divided me,
One half of me is yours, the other half yours—
Mine own I would say: but if mine then yours,
And so all yours. O, these naughty times
Put bars between the owners and their rights,
20 And so though yours, not yours. Prove it so—
Let Fortune go to hell for it, not I.
I speak too long, but 'tis to peise the time,
To eche it and to draw it out in length,
To stay you from election.
    Bassanio.   Let me choose,
For as I am, I live upon the rack.
    Portia. Upon the rack, Bassanio? then confess
What treason there is mingled with your love.
    Bassanio. None but that ugly treason of mistrust,
Which makes me fear th'enjoying of my love.
30 There may as well be amity and life
'Tween snow and fire, as treason and my love.
    Portia. Ay, but I fear you speak upon the rack,
Where men enforcéd do speak any thing.
    Bassanio. Promise me life, and I'll confess the truth.
    Portia. Well then, confess and live.
    Bassanio.   'Confess' and 'love
Had been the very sum of my confession:
O happy torment, when my torturer
Doth teach me answers for deliverance.
But let me to my fortune and the caskets.
40   *Portia.* Away then! I am locked in one of them—
If you do love me, you will find me out.
Nerissa and the rest, stand all aloof.

Let music sound while he doth make his choice—
Then if he lose, he makes a swan-like end,
Fading in music. [*all but the servitor go up into the gallery*
                   That the comparison
May stand more proper, my eye shall be the stream,
And wat'ry death-bed for him. He may win,
And what is music then? then music is
Even as the flourish when true subjects bow
To a new-crownéd monarch: such it is,   50
As are those dulcet sounds in break of day
That creep into the dreaming bridegroom's ear,
And summon him to marriage. Now he goes,
With no less presence, but with much more love;
Than young Alcides, when he did redeem
The virgin tribute paid by howling Troy
To the sea-monster. I stand for sacrifice:
The rest aloof are the Dardanian wives,
With blearéd visages, come forth to view
The issue of th'exploit. Go, Hercules!   60
Live thou, I live. With much much more dismay
I view the fight than thou that mak'st the fray.

'*A song, the whilst* BASSANIO *comments on the caskets
                   to himself*'

          Tell me where is Fancy bred,
          Or in the heart, or in the head?
          How begot, how nourishéd?
All. Reply, reply.

          It is engendred in the eyes,
          With gazing fed, and Fancy dies
          In the cradle where it lies.
          Let us all ring Fancy's knell: 70
              I'll begin it—Ding, dong, bell.
All. Ding, dong, bell.

Bassanio. So may the outward shows be least themselves—
The world is still deceived with ornament.
In law, what plea so tainted and corrupt,
But, being seasoned with a gracious voice,
Obscures the show of evil? In religion,
What damnéd error, but some sober brow
Will bless it, and approve it with a text,
80 Hiding the grossness with fair ornament?
There is no vice so simple, but assumes
Some mark of virtue on his outward parts:
How many cowards, whose hearts are all as false
As stairs of sand, wear yet upon their chins
The beards of Hercules and frowning Mars;
Who, inward searched, have livers white as milk?
And these assume but valour's excrement
To render them redoubted. Look on beauty,
And you shall see 'tis purchased by the weight,
90 Which therein works a miracle in nature,
Making them lightest that wear most of it:
So are those crispéd snaky golden locks
Which make such wanton gambols with the wind,
Upon supposéd fairness, often known
To be the dowry of a second head,
The skull that bred them in the sepulchre.
Thus ornament is but the guiléd shore
To a most dangerous sea; the beauteous scarf
Veiling an Indian beauty; in a word,
100 The seeming truth which cunning times put on
To entrap the wisest. Therefore, thou gaudy gold,
Hard food for Midas, I will none of thee—
Nor none of thee, thou pale and common drudge
'Tween man and man: but thou, thou meagre lead,
Which rather threaten'st than dost promise aught,
Thy plainness moves me more than eloquence,

And here choose I—joy be the consequence!

                              [the servitor gives him the key

(*Portia.* How all the other passions fleet to air,
As doubtful thoughts, and rash-embraced despair,
And shudd'ring fear and green-eyed jealousy!   110
O love, be moderate, allay thy ecstasy,
In measure rain thy joy, scant this excess—
I feel too much thy blessing, make it less,
For fear I surfeit!

  Bassanio [*opens the leaden casket*]. What find I here?
Fair Portia's counterfeit! What demi-god
Hath come so near creation? Move these eyes?
Or whether, riding on the balls of mine,
Seem they in motion? Here are severed lips,
Parted with sugar breath—so sweet a bar
Should sunder such sweet friends. Here in her hairs   120
The painter plays the spider, and hath woven
A golden mesh t'entrap the hearts of men,
Faster than gnats in cobwebs—But her eyes!
How could he see to do them? having made one,
Methinks it should have power to steal both his,
And leave itself unfurnished: yet look, how far
The substance of my praise doth wrong this shadow
In underprizing it, so far this shadow
Doth limp behind the substance. Here's the scroll,
The continent and summary of my fortune.   130

       'You that choose not by the view
         Chance as fair and choose as true:
         Since this fortune falls to you,
         Be content, and seek no new.
         If you be well pleased with this,
         And hold your fortune for your bliss,
         Turn you where your lady is,
         And claim her with a loving kiss.'

A gentle scroll...[*he turns to Portia*] Fair lady, by
    your leave,
140 I come by note, to give and to receive.
Like one of two contending in a prize,
That thinks he hath done well in people's eyes,
Hearing applause and universal shout,
Giddy in spirit, still gazing in a doubt
Whether those peals of praise be his or no,
So thrice-fair lady stand I, even so,
As doubtful whether what I see be true,
Until confirmed, signed, ratified by you.
    Portia. You see me, Lord Bassanio, where I stand,
150 Such as I am. Though for myself alone
I would not be ambitious in my wish
To wish myself much better, yet for you
I would be trebled twenty times myself—
A thousand times more fair, ten thousand times
More rich.
That only to stand high in your account,
I might in virtues, beauties, livings, friends,
Exceed account. But the full sum of me
Is some of something which, to term in gross,
160 Is an unlessoned girl, unschooled, unpractised,
Happy in this, she is not yet so old
But she may learn; happier than this,
She is not bred so dull but she can learn;
Happiest of all is that her gentle spirit
Commits itself to yours to be directed,
As from her lord, her governor, her king.... [*they kiss*
Myself and what is mine to you and yours
Is now converted. But now I was the lord
Of this fair mansion, master of my servants,
170 Queen o'er myself; and even now, but now,
This house, these servants, and this same myself,

Are yours—my lord's!—I give them with this ring,
Which when you part from, lose, or give away,
Let it presage the ruin of your love,
And be my vantage to exclaim on you.
  Bassanio. Madam, you have bereft me of all words,
Only my blood speaks to you in my veins,
And there is such confusion in my powers,
As after some oration fairly spoke
By a belovéd prince there doth appear   180
Among the buzzing pleaséd multitude,
Where every something, being blent together,
Turns to a wild of nothing, save of joy,
Expressed and not expressed. But when this ring
Parts from this finger, then parts life from hence!
O, then be bold to say Bassanio's dead.

        NERISSA and GRATIANO descend

  Nerissa. My lord and lady, it is now our time,
That have stood by and seen our wishes prosper,
To cry 'good joy.' Good joy, my lord, and lady!
  Gratiano. My Lord Bassanio, and my gentle lady, 190
I wish you all the joy that you can wish;
For I am sure you can wish none from me:
And, when your honours mean to solemnize
The bargain of your faith, I do beseech you,
Even at that time I may be married too.
  Bassanio. With all my heart, so thou canst get a wife.
  Gratiano. I thank your lordship, you have got
      me one.   *[he takes Nerissa by the hand*
My eyes, my lord, can look as swift as yours:
You saw the mistress, I beheld the maid;
You loved, I loved—for intermission   200
No more pertains to me, my lord, than you;
Your fortune stood upon the caskets there,

And so did mine too, as the matter falls:
For wooing here until I sweat again,
And swearing till my very roof was dry
With oaths of love, at last—if promise last—
I got a promise of this fair one here,
To have her love, provided that your fortune
Achieved her mistress.

    Portia.   Is this true, Nerissa?

210 *Nerissa.* Madam, it is, so you stand pleased withal.

    Bassanio. And do you, Gratiano, mean good faith?

    Gratiano. Yes, faith, my lord.

    Bassanio. Our feast shall be much honoured in
        your marriage.

    Gratiano. We'll play with them the first boy for a
thousand ducats.

    Nerissa. What! and stake down?

    Gratiano. No, we shall ne'er win at that sport, and
stake down.

LORENZO, JESSICA, and SALERIO enter the chamber

But who comes here? Lorenzo and his infidel?
220 What, and my old Venetian friend, Salerio?

    Bassanio. Lorenzo and Salerio, welcome hither,
If that the youth of my new interest here
Have power to bid you welcome...[*to Portia*] By
        your leave,
I bid my very friends and countrymen,
Sweet Portia, welcome.

    Portia.   So do I, my lord.
They are entirely welcome.

    Lorenzo. I thank your honour. For my part, my lord,
My purpose was not to have seen you here,
But meeting with Salerio by the way,
230 He did entreat me, past all saying nay,

To come with him along.

Salerio.   I did, my lord,
And I have reason for it. Signior Antonio
Commends him to you.   *[he gives Bassanio a letter*

Bassanio.   Ere I ope his letter,
I pray you, tell me how my good friend doth.

Salerio. Not sick, my lord, unless it be in mind—
Nor well, unless in mind: his letter there
Will show you his estate.   *[Bassanio opens the letter*

Gratiano. Nerissa, cheer yon stranger, bid
        her welcome....

                [Nerissa greets Jessica; Gratiano salutes Salerio
Your hand, Salerio. What's the news from Venice?
How doth that royal merchant, good Antonio?   *[aside* 240
I know he will be glad of our success,
We are the Jasons, we have won the fleece!

Salerio. I would you had won the fleece that he
        hath lost.   *[they talk apart*

Portia. There are some shrewd contents in yon
        same paper,
That steals the colour from Bassanio's cheek—
Some dear friend dead, else nothing in the world
Could turn so much the constitution
Of any constant man. What, worse and worse!
                        [she lays her hand upon his arm
With leave, Bassanio—I am half yourself,
And I must freely have the half of anything   250
That this same paper brings you.

Bassanio.   O sweet Portia,
Here are a few of the unpleasant'st words,
That ever blotted paper.   Gentle lady,
When I did first impart my love to you,
I freely told you all the wealth I had
Ran in my veins—I was a gentleman—

And then I told you true: and yet, dear lady,
Rating myself at nothing, you shall see
How much I was a braggart. When I told you
260 My state was nothing, I should then have told you
That I was worse than nothing; for, indeed,
I have engaged myself to a dear friend,
Engaged my friend to his mere enemy,
To feed my means....[*with breaking voice*] Here is a
    letter, lady,
The paper as the body of my friend,
And every word in it a gaping wound,
Issuing life-blood. But is it true, Salerio?
Have all his ventures failed? What, not one hit?
From Tripolis, from Mexico, and England,
270 From Lisbon, Barbary, and India?
And not one vessel scape the dreadful touch
Of merchant-marring rocks?
  Salerio.   Not one, my lord.
Besides, it should appear, that if he had
The present money to discharge the Jew,
He would not take it: never did I know
A creature that did bear the shape of man
So keen and greedy to confound a man.
He plies the duke at morning and at night,
And doth impeach the freedom of the state,
280 If they deny him justice. Twenty merchants,
The duke himself, and the magnificoes
Of greatest port, have all persuaded with him,
But none can drive him from the envious plea
Of forfeiture, of justice, and his bond.
  Jessica. When I was with him, I have heard
    him swear
To Tubal and to Chus, his countrymen,
That he would rather have Antonio's flesh

Than twenty times the value of the sum
That he did owe him: and I know, my lord,
If law, authority, and power deny not,   290
It will go hard with poor Antonio.

  Portia. Is it your dear friend that is thus in trouble?

  Bassanio. The dearest friend to me, the kindest man,
The best-conditioned and unwearied spirit
In doing courtesies: and one in whom
The ancient Roman honour more appears
Than any that draws breath in Italy.

  Portia. What sum owes he the Jew?

  Bassanio. For me, three thousand ducats.

  Portia.   What, no more?
Pay him six thousand, and deface the bond;   300
Double six thousand, and then treble that,
Before a friend of this description
Shall lose a hair thorough Bassanio's fault.
First, go with me to church, and call me wife,
And then away to Venice to your friend;
For never shall you lie by Portia's side
With an unquiet soul! You shall have gold
To pay the petty debt twenty times over.
When it is paid, bring your true friend along.
My maid Nerissa and myself meantime   310
Will live as maids and widows...Come, away!
For you shall hence upon your wedding-day:
Bid your friends welcome, show a merry cheer,
Since you are dear bought, I will love you dear.
But let me hear the letter of your friend.

  Bassanio [*reads*]. 'Sweet Bassanio, my ships have all
miscarried, my creditors grow cruel, my estate is very
low, my bond to the Jew is forfeit, and since, in paying
it, it is impossible I should live, all debts are cleared
between you and I, if I might but see you at my death: 320

notwithstanding, use your pleasure—if your love do
not persuade you to come, let not my letter.'

Portia. O love, dispatch all business and be gone!

Bassanio. Since I have your good leave to go away,
  I will make haste; but, till I come again,
No bed shall e'er be guilty of my stay,
  No rest be interposer 'twixt us twain.

                                  [*they hurry forth*

[3.3.]   *The street before Shylock's house*

SHYLOCK (*at his door*), SOLANIO, ANTONIO,
                and a Gaoler

Shylock. Gaoler, look to him—tell not me of mercy—
This is the fool that lent out money gratis.
Gaoler, look to him.

Antonio.   Hear me yet, good Shylock.

Shylock. I'll have my bond, speak not against my bond,
I have sworn an oath that I will have my bond:
Thou call'dst me dog before thou hadst a cause,
But since I am a dog beware my fangs.
The duke shall grant me justice. I do wonder,
Thou naughty gaoler, that thou art so fond
10 To come abroad with him at his request.

Antonio. I pray thee, hear me speak.

Shylock.   I'll have my bond—I will not hear
        thee speak.
I'll have my bond, and therefore speak no more.
I'll not be made a soft and dull-eyed fool,
To shake the head, relent, and sigh, and yield
To Christian intercessors. Follow not—
I'll have no speaking, I will have my bond.

            [*he goes within, slamming the door behind him*

Solanio. It is the most impenetrable cur,
That ever kept with men.

Antonio.   Let him alone,
I'll follow him no more with bootless prayers.   20
He seeks my life—his reason well I know;
I oft delivered from his forfeitures
Many that have at times made moan to me.
Therefore he hates me.

Solanio.   I am sure, the duke
Will never grant this forfeiture to hold.

Antonio. The duke cannot deny the course of law:
For the commodity that strangers have
With us in Venice, if it be denied,
Will much impeach the justice of the state,
Since that the trade and profit of the city   30
Consisteth of all nations.   Therefore, go.
These griefs and losses have so bated me,
That I shall hardly spare a pound of flesh
To-morrow to my bloody creditor.
Well, gaoler, on. Pray God, Bassanio come
To see me pay his debt, and then I care not!   [*they go*

[3.4.]   *The hall of Portia's house at Belmont*

PORTIA, NERISSA, LORENZO, JESSICA, *and a man
of Portia's, called* BALTHAZAR

Lorenzo. Madam, although I speak it in your presence,
You have a noble and a true conceit
Of god-like amity, which appears most strongly
In bearing thus the absence of your lord.
But if you knew to whom you show this honour,
How true a gentleman you send relief,
How dear a lover of my lord your husband,

I know you would be prouder of the work,
Than customary bounty can enforce you.

10 *Portia.* I never did repent for doing good,
Nor shall not now: for in companions
That do converse and waste the time together,
Whose souls do bear an egall yoke of love,
There must be needs a like proportion
Of lineaments, of manners, and of spirit;
Which makes me think that this Antonio,
Being the bosom lover of my lord,
Must needs be like my lord. If it be so,
How little is the cost I have bestowed

20 In purchasing the semblance of my soul
From out the state of hellish cruelty?
This comes too near the praising of myself,
Therefore no more of it: hear other things.
Lorenzo, I commit into your hands
The husbandry and manage of my house,
Until my lord's return: for mine own part,
I have toward heaven breathed a secret vow
To live in prayer and contemplation,
Only attended by Nerissa here,

30 Until her husband and my lord's return.
There is a monastery two miles off,
And there we will abide. I do desire you
Not to deny this imposition,
The which my love and some necessity
Now lays upon you.

 Lorenzo [*bows*]. Madam, with all my heart
I shall obey you in all fair commands.

 Portia. My people do already know my mind,
And will acknowledge you and Jessica
In place of Lord Bassanio and myself.

40 So fare you well till we shall meet again.

 Lorenzo. Fair thoughts and happy hours attend on you!

Jessica. I wish your ladyship all heart's content.

Portia. I thank you for your wish, and am
    well pleased
To wish it back on you: fare you well, Jessica....
                              [*Jessica and Lorenzo go out*
Now, Balthazar,
As I have ever found thee honest-true,
So let me find thee still. Take this same letter,
And use thou all th'endeavour of a man
In speed to Padua; see thou render this
Into my cousin's hand, Doctor Bellario,   50
And look what notes and garments he doth give thee,
Bring them, I pray thee, with imagined speed
†Unto the tranect, to the common ferry
Which trades to Venice. Waste no time in words,
But get thee gone. I shall be there before thee.

Balthazar. Madam, I go with all convenient speed.
                              [*he departs*

Portia. Come on, Nerissa—I have work in hand
That you yet know not of; we'll see our husbands
Before they think of us!

Nerissa.   Shall they see us?

Portia. They shall, Nerissa; but in such a habit,   60
That they shall think we are accomplishéd
With that we lack. I'll hold thee any wager,
When we are both accoutred like young men,
I'll prove the prettier fellow of the two,
And wear my dagger with the braver grace,
And speak between the change of man and boy
With a reed-voice, and turn two mincing steps
Into a manly stride; and speak of frays
Like a fine bragging youth; and tell quaint lies,
How honourable ladies sought my love,   70
Which I denying, they fell sick and died—
I could not do withal! Then I'll repent,

And wish, for all that, that I had not killed them.
And twenty of these puny lies I'll tell,
That men shall swear I have discontinued school
Above a twelvemonth. I have within my mind
A thousand raw tricks of these bragging Jacks,
Which I will practise.

    Nerissa.   Why, shall we turn to men?

    Portia. Fie, what a question's that,
80 If thou wert near a lewd interpreter!
But come, I'll tell thee all my whole device,
When I am in my coach, which stays for us
At the park-gate; and therefore haste away,
For we must measure twenty miles to-day.

                                  [they hurry forth

[3.5.] *An avenue of trees leading up to Portia's house;
on either side, grassy banks and lawns set with cypresses*

LANCELOT *and* JESSICA *approach in conversation*

    Lancelot. Yes truly, for look you, the sins of the
father are to be laid upon the children—therefore, I
promise you, I fear you. I was always plain with you,
and so now I speak my agitation of the matter: therefore,
be o' good cheer, for truly I think you are damned. There
is but one hope in it that can do you any good, and that
is but a kind of bastard hope neither.

    Jessica. And what hope is that, I pray thee?

    Lancelot. Marry, you may partly hope that your
10 father got you not, that you are not the Jew's daughter.

    Jessica. That were a kind of bastard hope, indeed!
So the sins of my mother should be visited upon me.

    Lancelot. Truly then I fear you are damned both by
father and mother: thus when I shun Scylla, your

father, I fall into Charybdis, your mother: well, you are gone both ways.

Jessica. I shall be saved by my husband—he hath made me a Christian.

Lancelot. Truly, the more to blame he. We were Christians enow before, e'en as many as could well 20 live, one by another. This making of Christians will raise the price of hogs—if we grow all to be pork-eaters, we shall not shortly have a rasher on the coals for money.

LORENZO *is seen coming from the house*

Jessica. I'll tell my husband, Lancelot, what you say—here he comes.

Lorenzo. I shall grow jealous of you shortly, Lancelot, if you thus get my wife into corners.

Jessica. Nay, you need not fear us, Lorenzo. Lancelot and I are out. He tells me flatly there's no mercy for me in heaven, because I am a Jew's daughter: and 30 he says you are no good member of the commonwealth, for, in converting Jews to Christians, you raise the price of pork.

Lorenzo. I shall answer that better to the commonwealth than you can the getting up of the negro's belly: the Moor is with child by you, Lancelot.

Lancelot. It is much that the Moor should be more than reason: but if she be less than an honest woman, she is indeed more than I took her for.

Lorenzo. How every fool can play upon the word! 40 I think the best grace of wit will shortly turn into silence, and discourse grow commendable in none only but parrots. Go in, sirrah—bid them prepare for dinner.

Lancelot. That is done, sir—they have all stomachs.

Lorenzo. Goodly Lord, what a wit-snapper are you! then bid them prepare dinner.

Lancelot. That is done too, sir—only 'cover' is the word.

Lorenzo. Will you cover then, sir?

50 *Lancelot.* Not so, sir, neither—I know my duty.

Lorenzo. Yet more quarrelling with occasion! Wilt thou show the whole wealth of thy wit in an instant? I pray thee, understand a plain man in his plain meaning: go to thy fellows, bid them cover the table, serve in the meat, and we will come in to dinner.

Lancelot. For the table, sir, it shall be served in— for the meat, sir, it shall be covered—for your coming in to dinner, sir, why, let it be as humours and conceits shall govern. *[he goes within*

60 *Lorenzo.* O dear discretion, how his words are suited!
The fool hath planted in his memory
An army of good words, and I do know
A many fools that stand in better place
Garnished like him, that for a tricksy word
Defy the matter. How cheer'st thou, Jessica?
And now, good sweet, say thy opinion,
How dost thou like the Lord Bassanio's wife?

Jessica. Past all expressing. It is very meet,
The Lord Bassanio live an upright life,
70 For having such a blessing in his lady
He finds the joys of heaven here on earth,
And if on earth he do not merit it,
In reason he should never come to heaven!
Why, if two gods should play some heavenly match,
And on the wager lay two earthly women,
And Portia one, there must be something else
Pawned with the other, for the poor rude world
Hath not her fellow.

Lorenzo. Even such a husband
Hast thou of me, as she is for a wife.

Jessica. Nay, but ask my opinion too of that.   80

Lorenzo. I will anon—first, let us go to dinner.

Jessica. Nay, let me praise you while I have
 a stomach.

Lorenzo. No, pray thee, let it serve for table-talk—
Then, howsome'er thou speak'st, 'mong other things
I shall digest it.

Jessica.   Well, I'll set you forth.

          [they go in to dinner

[4.1.] *A Court of Justice; on a platform at the back
a great chair of state with three lower chairs on either
side; before these a table for clerks, lawyers' desks, etc.*

*A*NTONIO *(guarded),* B*ASSANIO,* G*RATIANO,* S*OLANIO,*
*officers, clerks, attendants, and a concourse of people. The
D*UKE *in white and six* M*agnificoes in red enter in state
and take their seats*

Duke. What, is Antonio here?

Antonio. Ready, so please your grace.

Duke. I am sorry for thee—thou art come to answer
A stony adversary, an inhuman wretch
Uncapable of pity, void and empty
From any dram of mercy.

Antonio.   I have heard,
Your grace hath ta'en great pains to qualify
His rigorous course; but since he stands obdúrate,
And that no lawful means can carry me
Out of his envy's reach, I do oppose   10
My patience to his fury, and am armed
To suffer with a quietness of spirit
The very tyranny and rage of his.

Duke. Go one, and call the Jew into the court.

Solanio. He is ready at the door, he comes, my lord.

Duke. Make room, and let him stand before
 our face.

The crowd parts, and SHYLOCK *confronts the Duke;*
he bows low

Shylock, the world thinks, and I think so too,
That thou but leadest this fashion of thy malice
To the last hour of act, and then 'tis thought
20 Thou'lt show thy mercy and remorse more strange
Than is thy strange apparent cruelty;
And where thou now exacts the penalty,
Which is a pound of this poor merchant's flesh,
Thou wilt not only loose the forfeiture,
But touched with human gentleness and love,
Forgive a moiety of the principal;
Glancing an eye of pity on his losses,
That have of late so huddled on his back;
Enow to press a royal merchant down,
30 And pluck commiseration of his state
From brassy bosoms and rough hearts of flint,
From stubborn Turks and Tartars, never trained
To offices of tender courtesy.
We all expect a gentle answer, Jew.
 Shylock. I have possessed your grace of what I purpose,
And by our holy Sabbath have I sworn
To have the due and forfeit of my bond.
If you deny it, let the danger light
Upon your charter and your city's freedom!
40 You'll ask me why I rather choose to have
A weight of carrion flesh than to receive
Three thousand ducats: I'll not answer that!
But say it is my humour, is it answered?
What if my house be troubled with a rat,
And I be pleased to give ten thousand ducats

To have it baned? what, are you answered yet?
Some men there are love not a gaping pig,
Some that are mad if they behold a cat,
And others when the bag-pipe sings i'th' nose
Cannot contain their urine: for affection,   50
Mistress of passion, sways it to the mood
Of what it likes or loathes. Now, for your answer:
As there is no firm reason to be rendred,
Why he cannot abide a gaping pig;
Why he, a harmless necessary cat;
Why he, a woollen bag-pipe; but of force
Must yield to such inevitable shame,
As to offend, himself being offended;
So can I give no reason, nor I will not,
More than a lodged hate and a certain loathing   60
I bear Antonio, that I follow thus
A losing suit against him! Are you answered?
 Bassanio. This is no answer, thou unfeeling man,
To excuse the current of thy cruelty!
 Shylock. I am not bound to please thee with
     my answers!
 Bassanio. Do all men kill the things they do not love?
 Shylock. Hates any man the thing he would not kill?
 Bassanio. Every offence is not a hate at first!
 Shylock. What, wouldst thou have a serpent sting
     thee twice?
 Antonio. I pray you, think you question with the Jew 70
You may as well go stand upon the beach
And bid the main flood bate his usual height;
You may as well use question with the wolf
Why he hath made the ewe bleat for the lamb;
You may as well forbid the mountain pines
To wag their high tops and to make no noise
When they are fretten with the gusts of heaven;

Q.M.V. – 6

You may as well do any thing most hard,
As seek to soften that—than which what's harder?—
His Jewish heart. Therefore, I do beseech you,
Make no moe offers, use no farther means,
But with all brief and plain conveniency
Let me have judgement and the Jew his will!

   Bassanio. For thy three thousand ducats here is six.
   Shylock. If every ducat in six thousand ducats
Were in six parts and every part a ducat,
I would not draw them, I would have my bond!
   Duke. How shalt thou hope for mercy, rendring none?
   Shylock. What judgement shall I dread, doing
     no wrong?
You have among you many a purchased slave,
Which, like your asses and your dogs and mules,
You use in abject and in slavish parts,
Because you bought them—shall I say to you,
'Let them be free, marry them to your heirs?
Why sweat they under burthens? let their beds
Be made as soft as yours, and let their palates
Be seasoned with such viands?' You will answer,
'The slaves are ours.' So do I answer you:
The pound of flesh, which I demand of him
Is dearly bought, 'tis mine, and I will have it:
If you deny me, fie upon your law!
There is no force in the decrees of Venice!
I stand for judgement. Answer—shall I have it?
   Duke. Upon my power, I may dismiss this court,
Unless Bellario, a learned doctor,
Whom I have sent for to determine this,
Come here to-day.
   Solanio.   My lord, here stays without
A messenger with letters from the doctor,
New come from Padua.

Duke. Bring us the letters; call the messenger.   110
Bassanio. Good cheer, Antonio! what man, courage yet:
The Jew shall have my flesh, blood, bones, and all,
Ere thou shalt lose for me one drop of blood.
[*Shylock takes a knife from his girdle and kneels to whet it*
  Antonio. I am a tainted wether of the flock,
Meetest for death. The weakest kind of fruit
Drops earliest to the ground, and so let me;
You cannot better be employed, Bassanio,
Than to live still, and write mine epitaph.

    NERISSA *enters, dressed as a lawyer's clerk*

Duke. Came you from Padua, from Bellario?
Nerissa [*bows*]. From both, my lord. Bellario greets
      your grace.   120
      [*she presents a letter; the Duke opens and reads it*
Bassanio. Why dost thou whet thy knife so earnestly?
Shylock. To cut the forfeiture from that bankrupt there.
Gratiano. Not on thy sole, but on thy soul, harsh Jew,
Thou mak'st thy knife keen: but no metal can,
No, not the hangman's axe, bear half the keenness
Of thy sharp envy: can no prayers pierce thee?
  Shylock. No, none that thou hast wit enough to make.
  Gratiano. O, be thou damned, inexorable dog,
And for thy life let justice be accused!
Thou almost mak'st me waver in my faith,   130
To hold opinion with Pythagoras
That souls of animals infuse themselves
Into the trunks of men: thy currish spirit
Governed a Wolf, who hanged for human slaughter,
Even from the gallows did his fell soul fleet,
And whilst thou layest in thy unhallowed dam,
Infused itself in thee; for thy desires
Are wolvish, bloody, starved, and ravenous.

Shylock. Till thou canst rail the seal from off my bond,
140 Thou but offend'st thy lungs to speak so loud:
Repair thy wit, good youth, or it will fall
To cureless ruin. I stand here for law.
Duke. This letter from Bellario doth commend
A young and learned doctor to our court:
Where is he?
Nerissa. He attendeth here hard by
To know your answer, whether you'll admit him.
Duke. With all my heart: some three or four of you,
Go give him courteous conduct to this place.

[*attendants bow and depart*

Meantime, the court shall hear Bellario's letter....

He reads out the letter

150 'Your grace shall understand that at the receipt of your
letter I am very sick, but in the instant that your messenger came, in loving visitation was with me a young doctor
of Rome, his name is Balthazar. I acquainted him with
the cause in controversy between the Jew and Antonio
the merchant; we turned oe'r many books together; he
is furnished with my opinion, which bettered with his
own learning, the greatness whereof I cannot enough
commend, comes with him at my importunity to fill up
your grace's request in my stead. I beseech you, let his
160 lack of years be no impediment to let him lack a reverend
estimation, for I never knew so young a body with so
old a head. I leave him to your gracious acceptance,
whose trial shall better publish his commendation.'
You hear the learned Bellario, what he writes.

PORTIA enters, dressed as a doctor of civil law,
with a book in her hand

And here, I take it, is the doctor come.
Give me your hand. Come you from old Bellario?

Portia. I did, my lord.

Duke.   You are welcome. Take your place...

[*an attendant ushers Portia to a desk near the Duke*

Are you acquainted with the difference
That holds this present question in the court?

Portia. I am informéd throughly of the cause.   170
Which is the merchant here, and which the Jew?

Duke. Antonio and old Shylock, both stand forth.

[*they step forward and bow to the Duke*

Portia. Is your name Shylock?

Shylock.   Shylock is my name.

Portia. Of a strange nature is the suit you follow,
Yet in such rule that the Venetian law
Cannot impugn you as you do proceed.
You stand within his danger, do you not?

Antonio. Ay, so he says.

Portia.   Do you confess the bond?

Antonio. I do.

Portia.   Then must the Jew be merciful.

Shylock. On what compulsion must I? tell me that.   180

Portia. The quality of mercy is not strained,
It droppeth as the gentle rain from heaven
Upon the place beneath. It is twice blessed:
It blesseth him that gives, and him that takes,
'Tis mightiest in the mightiest, it becomes
The thronéd monarch better than his crown:
His sceptre shows the force of temporal power,
The attribute to awe and majesty,
Wherein doth sit the dread and fear of kings:
But mercy is above this sceptred sway,   190
It is enthronéd in the hearts of kings,
It is an attribute to God himself;
And earthly power doth then show likest God's,
When mercy seasons justice. Therefore, Jew,

Though justice be thy plea, consider this,
That in the course of justice none of us
Should see salvation: we do pray for mercy,
And that same prayer doth teach us all to render
The deeds of mercy.   I have spoke thus much,
200 To mitigate the justice of thy plea,
Which if thou follow, this strict court of Venice
Must needs give sentence 'gainst the merchant there.
   Shylock. My deeds upon my head! I crave the law,
The penalty and forfeit of my bond.
   Portia. Is he not able to discharge the money?
   Bassanio. Yes, here I tender it for him in the court,
Yea, twice the sum. If that will not suffice,
I will be bound to pay it ten times o'er,
On forfeit of my hands, my head, my heart.
210 If this will not suffice, it must appear
That malice bears down truth.   [*he kneels with hands
         uplifted*] And I beseech you,
Wrest once the law to your authority—
To do a great right, do a little wrong,
And curb this cruel devil of his will.
   Portia. It must not be, there is no power in Venice
Can alter a decree establishéd:
'Twill be recorded for a precedent,
And many an error by the same example
Will rush into the state. It cannot be.
220 *Shylock*. A Daniel come to judgement: yea,
         a Daniel!   [*he kisses the hem of her robe*
O wise young judge, how I do honour thee!
   Portia. I pray you, let me look upon the bond.
   Shylock [*swiftly snatching a paper from his bosom*]. Here
      'tis, most reverend doctor, here it is.
   Portia [*taking the paper*]. Shylock, there's thrice thy
      money offered thee.

Shylock. An oath, an oath, I have an oath in heaven.
Shall I lay perjury upon my soul?
No, not for Venice.

  Portia [*perusing the paper*]. Why, this bond is forfeit,
And lawfully by this the Jew may claim
A pound of flesh, to be by him cut off
Nearest the merchant's heart. Be merciful,   230
Take thrice thy money, bid me tear the bond.

  Shylock. When it is paid according to the tenour.
It doth appear you are a worthy judge,
You know the law, your exposition
Hath been most sound: I charge you by the law,
Whereof you are a well-deserving pillar,
Proceed to judgement: by my soul I swear,
There is no power in the tongue of man
To alter me. I stay here on my bond.

  Antonio. Most heartily I do beseech the court   240
To give the judgement.

  Portia.   Why then, thus it is.
You must prepare your bosom for his knife.

  Shylock. O noble judge! O excellent young man!

  Portia. For the intent and purpose of the law
Hath full relation to the penalty,
Which here appeareth due upon the bond.

  Shylock. 'Tis very true: O wise and upright judge!
How much more elder art thou than thy looks!

  Portia. Therefore, lay bare your bosom.

  Shylock.   Ay, his breast,
So says the bond, doth it not, noble judge?   250
'Nearest his heart,' those are the very words.

  Portia. It is so. Are there balance here, to weigh
The flesh?

  Shylock.   I have them ready.
                [*he opens his cloak and takes them out*

Portia. Have by some surgeon, Shylock, on your charge,
To stop his wounds, lest he do bleed to death.
Shylock. Is it so nominated in the bond?
                                    [*he takes it and examines it closely*
Portia. It is not so expressed, but what of that?
'Twere good you do so much for charity
Shylock. I cannot find it, 'tis not in the bond.
                                    [*he gives it back to Portia*
260 *Portia.* You merchant, have you any thing to say?
Antonio. But little; I am armed and well prepared.
Give me your hand, Bassanio, fare you well!
Grieve not that I am fall'n to this for you;
For herein Fortune shows herself more kind
Than is her custom: it is still her use,
To let the wretched man outlive his wealth,
To view with hollow eye and wrinkled brow
An age of poverty; from which ling'ring penance
Of such misery doth she cut me off.   [*they embrace*
270 Commend me to your honourable wife,
Tell her the process of Antonio's end,
Say how I loved you, speak me fair in death;
And when the tale is told, bid her be judge
Whether Bassanio had not once a love.
Repent but you that you shall lose your friend,
And he repents not, that he pays your debt.
For if the Jew do cut but deep enough,
I'll pay it instantly with all my heart.
Bassanio. Antonio, I am married to a wife
280 Which is as dear to me as life itself,
But life itself, my wife, and all the world,
Are not with me esteemed above thy life.
I would lose all, ay, sacrifice them all
Here to this devil, to deliver you.
Portia. Your wife would give you little thanks
      for that,

If she were by, to hear you make the offer.

Gratiano. I have a wife, whom, I protest, I love—
I would she were in heaven, so she could
Entreat some power to change this currish Jew.

Nerissa. 'Tis well you offer it behind her back,   290
The wish would make else an unquiet house.

Shylock. These be the Christian husbands! I have
    a daughter—
Would any of the stock of Bárrabas
Had been her husband, rather than a Christian....
[*aloud*] We trifle time, I pray thee pursue sentence.

Portia. A pound of that same merchant's flesh
    is thine,
The court awards it, and the law doth give it.

Shylock. Most rightful judge!

Portia. And you must cut this flesh from off
    his breast,
The law allows it, and the court awards it.   300

Shylock. Most learnéd judge—a sentence—
    come, prepare.   [*he advances with knife drawn*

Portia. Tarry a little, there is something else.
This bond doth give thee here no jot of blood—
The words expressly are 'a pound of flesh':
Take then thy bond, take thou thy pound of flesh,
But, in the cutting it, if thou dost shed
One drop of Christian blood, thy lands and goods
Are by the laws of Venice confiscate
Unto the state of Venice.

Gratiano. O upright judge!—mark, Jew—O
    learnéd judge!   310

Shylock. Is that the law?

Portia [*opens her book*]. Thyself shalt see
    the act:
For, as thou urgest justice, be assured
Thou shalt have justice more than thou desir'st.

Gratiano. O learnéd judge!—mark, Jew—a
    learnéd judge!

Shylock. I take this offer then—pay the bond thrice,
And let the Christian go.

    Bassanio.   Here is the money.

    Portia.   Soft!
The Jew shall have all justice—soft, no haste—
He shall have nothing but the penalty.

    Gratiano. O Jew! an upright judge, a learnéd judge!

320   *Portia.* Therefore, prepare thee to cut off
    the flesh.
Shed thou no blood, nor cut thou less nor more
But just a pound of flesh: if thou tak'st more
Or less than a just pound, be it but so much
As makes it light or heavy in the substance,
Or the division of the twentieth part
Of one poor scruple, nay, if the scale do turn
But in the estimation of a hair,
Thou diest and all thy goods are confiscate.

    Gratiano. A second Daniel, a Daniel, Jew!

330 Now, infidel, I have you on the hip.

    Portia. Why doth the Jew pause? take thy forfeiture.

    Shylock. Give me my principal, and let me go.

    Bassanio. I have it ready for thee, here it is.

    Portia. He hath refused it in the open court,
He shall have merely justice and his bond.

    Gratiano. A Daniel, still say I, a second Daniel!
I thank thee, Jew, for teaching me that word.

    Shylock. Shall I not have barely my principal?

    Portia. Thou shalt have nothing but the forfeiture

340 To be so taken at thy peril, Jew.

    Shylock. Why then the devil give him good of it!
I'll stay no longer question.   [*he turns to go*

    Portia.   Tarry, Jew.

The law hath yet another hold on you....

[she reads from her book

It is enacted in the laws of Venice,
If it be proved against an alien,
That by direct or indirect attempts
He seek the life of any citizen,
The party 'gainst the which he doth contrive
Shall seize one half his goods, the other half
Comes to the privy coffer of the state,   350
And the offender's life lies in the mercy
Of the duke only, 'gainst all other voice.

[she closes the book

In which predicament, I say, thou stand'st:
For it appears by manifest proceeding,
That indirectly and directly too
Thou hast contrived against the very life
Of the defendant; and thou hast incurred
The danger formerly by me rehearsed.
Down, therefore, and beg mercy of the duke.

   Gratiano. Beg that thou mayst have leave to
      hang thyself,   360
And yet thy wealth being forfeit to the state,
Thou hast not left the value of a cord,
Therefore thou must be hanged at the state's charge.

   Duke. That thou shalt see the difference of our spirit,
I pardon thee thy life before thou ask it:
For half thy wealth, it is Antonio's—
The other half comes to the general state,
Which humbleness may drive unto a fine.

   Portia. Ay, for the state, not for Antonio.

   Shylock. Nay, take my life and all, pardon not that.   370
You take my house, when you do take the prop
That doth sustain my house; you take my life,
When you do take the means whereby I live.

Portia. What mercy can you render him, Antonio?

Gratiano. A halter gratis—nothing else, for God's sake.

Antonio. So please my lord the duke and all
    the court
To quit the fine for one half of his goods,.
I am content; so he will let me have
The other half in use, to render it
380 Upon his death unto the gentleman
That lately stole his daughter;.
Two things provided more, that, for this favour,
He presently become a Christian;
The other, that he do record a gift,
Here in the court, of all he dies possessed,
Unto his son Lorenzo and his daughter.

  Duke. He shall do this, or else I do recant
The pardon that I late pronouncéd here.

  Portia. Art thou contented, Jew? what dost
    thou say?

390 *Shylock.* I am content.

  Portia [*to Nerissa*].   Clerk, draw a deed of gift.

  Shylock. I pray you give me leave to go from hence,
I am not well, send the deed after me,
And I will sign it.

  Duke.   Get thee gone, but do it.

  Gratiano. In christ'ning thou shalt have two
    godfathers—
Had I been judge, thou shouldst have had ten more,
To bring thee to the gallows, not the font.

         [*Shylock totters out amid cries of execration*

  Duke [*rising*]. Sir, I entreat you home with me
    to dinner.

  Portia. I humbly do desire your grace of pardon,
I must away this night toward Padua,
400 And it is meet I presently set forth.

Duke. I am sorry that your leisure serves you not.

                         [he comes down from his throne

Antonio, gratify this gentleman,

For in my mind you are much bound to him.

                         [the Duke, the Magnificoes and their
                             train depart; the crowd disperses

Bassanio. Most worthy gentleman, I and my friend

Have by your wisdom been this day acquitted

Of grievous penalties, in lieu whereof,

Three thousand ducats, due unto the Jew,

We freely cope your courteous pains withal.

Antonio. And stand indebted, over and above,

In love and service to you evermore.   410

Portia. He is well paid that is well satisfied,

And I, delivering you, am satisfied,

And therein do account myself well paid.

My mind was never yet more mercenary.

                         [passing them with a bow

I pray you, know me when we meet again.

I wish you well, and so I take my leave.

Bassanio [*hasting after*]. Dear sir, of force I must
    attempt you further.

Take some remembrance of us, as a tribute,

Not as a fee: grant me two things, I pray you,

Not to deny me, and to pardon me.   420

Portia [*stops at the door*]. You press me far, and
    therefore I will yield.

Give me your gloves, I'll wear them for your sake.

                          [he doffs them

And, for your love, I'll take this ring from you—

Do not draw back your hand—I'll take no more,

And you in love shall not deny me this?

Bassanio. This ring, good sir—alas, it is a trifle—

I will not shame myself to give you this.

Portia. I will have nothing else but only this;
And now, methinks, I have a mind to it.

430 *Bassanio.* There's more depends on this than on
    the value.
The dearest ring in Venice will I give you,
And find it out by proclamation,
Only for this, I pray you, pardon me.
    Portia. I see, sir, you are liberal in offers.
You taught me first to beg, and now, methinks,
You teach me how a beggar should be answered.
    Bassanio. Good sir, this ring was given me by my wife,
And when she put it on, she made me vow
That I should neither sell nor give nor lose it.

440 *Portia.* That 'scuse serves many men to save
    their gifts.
And if your wife be not a mad-woman,
And know how well I have deserved this ring,
She would not hold out enemy for ever,
For giving it to me...Well, peace be with you!

[she sweeps out, Nerissa following

    Antonio. My Lord Bassanio, let him have the ring.
Let his deservings and my love withal
Be valued 'gainst your wife's commandment.
    Bassanio. Go, Gratiano, run and overtake him,
Give him the ring, and bring him if thou canst
450 Unto Antonio's house—away, make haste.

[Gratiano hurries forth

Come, you and I will thither presently,
And in the morning early will we both
Fly toward Belmont. Come, Antonio.   *[they go*

[4.2.] *A street in Venice before the Court of Justice*

PORTIA *and* NERISSA *come from the Court*

Portia [*gives a paper*]. Inquire the Jew's house out,
    give him this deed,
And let him sign it. We'll away to-night,
And be a day before our husbands home:
This deed will be well welcome to Lorenzo.

GRATIANO *comes running from the Court*

Gratiano. Fair sir, you are well o'erta'en.
My Lord Bassanio, upon more advice,
Hath sent you here this ring, and doth entreat
Your company at dinner.
    Portia.   That cannot be:
His ring I do accept most thankfully,
And so I pray you tell him: furthermore,   10
I pray you, show my youth old Shylock's house.
    Gratiano. That will I do.
    Nerissa.   Sir, I would speak with you...
                      [*takes Portia aside*
I'll see if I can get my husband's ring,
Which I did make him swear to keep for ever.
    Portia. Thou mayst, I warrant. We shall have
    old swearing
That they did give the rings away to men;
But we'll outface them, and outswear them too.
Away, make haste, thou know'st where I will tarry.
    Nerissa [*turns to Gratiano*]. Come, good sir, will you
    show me to this house?   [*they go their ways*

[5.1.] *The avenue before Portia's house at Belmont;
    a summer night; a moon with drifting clouds*

LORENZO *and* JESSICA *pace softly beneath the trees*

Lorenzo. The moon shines bright. In such a night
    as this,
When the sweet wind did gently kiss the trees,
And they did make no noise, in such a night
Troilus methinks mounted the Troyan walls,
And sighed his soul toward the Grecian tents,
Where Cressid lay that night.
    Jessica.   In such a night
Did Thisbe fearfully o'ertrip the dew,
And saw the lion's shadow ere himself,
And ran dismayed away.
    Lorenzo.   In such a night
10 Stood Dido with a willow in her hand
    Upon the wild sea banks, and waft her love
    To come again to Carthage.
        Jessica.   In such a night
    Medea gathered the enchanted herbs
    That did renew old Æson.
        Lorenzo.   In such a night
    Did Jessica steal from the wealthy Jew,
    And with an unthrift love did run from Venice
    As far as Belmont.
        Jessica.   In such a night
    Did young Lorenzo swear he loved her well,
    Stealing her soul with many vows of faith,
20 And ne'er a true one.
        Lorenzo.   In such a night
    Did pretty Jessica (like a little shrew!)
    Slander her love, and he forgave it her.

Jessica. I would out-night you, did no body come:
But, hark, I hear the footing of a man.

STEPHANO *approaches, running*

Lorenzo. Who comes so fast in silence of the night?
Stephano. A friend.
Lorenzo. A friend! what friend? your name, I pray
　　you, friend?
Stephano. Stephano is my name, and I bring word
My mistress will before the break of day
Be here at Belmont—she doth stray about　　　　　30
By holy crosses, where she kneels and prays
For happy wedlock hours.
Lorenzo. 　　　　　　　　　Who comes with her?
Stephano. None, but a holy hermit and her maid.
I pray you, is my master yet returned?
Lorenzo. He is not, nor we have not heard from him.
But go we in, I pray thee, Jessica,
And ceremoniously let us prepare
Some welcome for the mistress of the house.

LANCELOT'S *voice heard hollaing at a distance*

Lancelot. Sola, sola! wo ha, ho, sola, sola!
Lorenzo. Who calls?　　　　　　　　　　　40
Lancelot [*running in and out of the trees*]. Sola!
did you see Master Lorenzo? Master Lorenzo? sola,
sola!
Lorenzo. Leave hollaing, man—here!
Lancelot. Sola! where? where?
Lorenzo. Here!
Lancelot. Tell him, there's a post come from my
master, with his horn full of good news. My master
will be here ere morning. 　　　　　　[*he runs off*

50 *Lorenzo.* Sweet soul, let's in, and there expect
  their coming.
 And yet no matter: why should we go in?
 My friend Stephano, signify, I pray you,
 Within the house, your mistress is at hand,
 And bring your music forth into the air.
       [Stephano goes within
 How sweet the moonlight sleeps upon this bank!
 Here will we sit and let the sounds of music
 Creep in our ears—soft stillness and the night
 Become the touches of sweet harmony. *[he sits*
 Sit, Jessica. Look how the floor of heaven
60 Is thick inlaid with patens of bright gold.
 There's not the smallest orb which thou behold'st
 But in his motion like an angel sings,
 Still choiring to the young-eyed cherubins;
 Such harmony is in immortal souls!
 But whilst this muddy vesture of decay
 Doth grossly close it in, we cannot hear it.

 Musicians steal from the house and bestow themselves
 among the trees; they leave the door open behind them,
 and a light shines therefrom

 Come, ho, and wake Diana with a hymn!
 With sweetest touches pierce your mistress' ear,
 And draw her home with music.   *[music*
70 *Jessica.* I am never merry when I hear
  sweet music.
 Lorenzo. The reason is, your spirits are attentive:
 For do but note a wild and wanton herd,
 Or race of youthful and unhandled colts,
 Fetching mad bounds, bellowing and neighing loud—
 Which is the hot condition of their blood—
 If they but hear perchance a trumpet sound,

Or any air of music touch their ears,
You shall perceive them make a mutual stand,
Their savage eyes turned to a modest gaze
By the sweet power of music: therefore, the poet   80
Did feign that Orpheus drew trees, stones, and floods,
Since nought so stockish, hard, and full of rage,
But music for the time doth change his nature.
The man that hath no music in himself,
Nor is not moved with concord of sweet sounds,
Is fit for treasons, stratagems, and spoils,
The motions of his spirit are dull as night,
And his affections dark as Erebus:
Let no such man be trusted.   Mark the music.

PORTIA and NERISSA come slowly along the avenue

Portia. That light we see is burning in my hall.   90
How far that little candle throws his beams!
So shines a good deed in a naughty world.
Nerissa. When the moon shone, we did not see
    the candle.
Portia. So doth the greater glory dim the less—
A substitute shines brightly as a king,
Until a king be by, and then his state
Empties itself, as doth an inland brook
Into the main of waters. Music! hark!
Nerissa. It is your music, madam, of the house.
Portia. Nothing is good, I see, without respect—   100
Methinks it sounds much sweeter than by day.
Nerissa. Silence bestows that virtue on it, madam.
Portia. The crow doth sing as sweetly as the lark
When neither is attended: and I think
The nightingale, if she should sing by day
When every goose is cackling, would be thought
No better a musician than the wren.

How many things by season seasoned are
To their right praise and true perfection.
110 Peace, ho! the moon sleeps with Endymion,
And would not be awaked.   [*the music ceases*

   Lorenzo.   That is the voice,
Or I am much deceived, of Portia.

   Portia. He knows me, as the blind man knows
      the cuckoo,
By the bad voice.

   Lorenzo.   Dear lady, welcome home.

   Portia. We have been praying for our husbands'
      welfare,
Which speed we hope the better for our words.
Are they returned?

   Lorenzo.   Madam, they are not yet;
But there is come a messenger before,
To signify their coming.

   Portia.   Go in, Nerissa,
120 Give order to my servants that they take
No note at all of our being absent hence—
Nor you, Lorenzo—Jessica, nor you.

                  [*'a tucket sounds'; voices are heard
                      at a distance in the avenue*

   Lorenzo. Your husband is at hand, I hear
      his trumpet.
We are no tell-tales, madam—fear you not.

   Portia. This night methinks is but the daylight sick,
It looks a little paler—'tis a day,
Such as the day is when the sun is hid.

'BASSANIO, ANTONIO, GRATIANO, and their followers'
come up

   Bassanio. We should hold day with the Antipodes,
If you would walk in absence of the sun.

Portia. Let me give light, but let me not be light,   130
For a light wife doth make a heavy husband,
And never be Bassanio so for me.
But God sort all.   You are welcome home, my lord.
                     [*Gratiano and Nerissa talk apart*

Bassanio. I thank you, madam. Give welcome to
    my friend—
This is the man, this is Antonio,
To whom I am so infinitely bound.

Portia. You should in all sense be much bound
    to him,
For, as I hear, he was much bound for you.

Antonio. No more than I am well acquitted of.

Portia. Sir, you are very welcome to our house: 140
It must appear in other ways than words,
Therefore I scant this breathing courtesy.

Gratiano. By yonder moon I swear you do me wrong,
In faith I gave it to the judge's clerk.
Would he were gelt that had it for my part,
Since you do take it, love, so much at heart.

Portia. A quarrel, ho, already! what's the matter?

Gratiano. About a hoop of gold, a paltry ring
That she did give to me, whose posy was
For all the world like cutler's poetry   150
Upon a knife, 'Love me, and leave me not.'

Nerissa. What talk you of the posy or the value?
You swore to me when I did give it you
That you would wear it till your hour of death,
And that it should lie with you in your grave.
Though not for me, yet for your vehement oaths,
You should have been respective and have kept it.
Gave it a judge's clerk! no, God's my judge,
The clerk will ne'er wear hair on's face that had it.

Gratiano. He will, an if he live to be a man.   160

Nerissa. Ay, if a woman live to be a man.

Gratiano. Now, by this hand, I gave it to a youth,
A kind of boy, a little scrubbéd boy,
No higher than thyself, the judge's clerk,
A prating boy, that begged it as a fee—
I could not for my heart deny it him.

Portia. You were to blame, I must be plain
        with you,
To part so slightly with your wife's first gift,
A thing stuck on with oaths upon your finger,
170 And riveted with faith unto your flesh.
I gave my love a ring, and made him swear
Never to part with it, and here he stands;
I dare be sworn for him he would not leave it,
Nor pluck it from his finger, for the wealth
That the world masters. Now, in faith, Gratiano,
You give your wife too unkind cause of grief.
An 'twere to me, I should be mad at it.

(*Bassanio.* Why, I were best to cut my left hand off,
And swear I lost the ring defending it.

180 *Gratiano.* My Lord Bassanio gave his ring away
Unto the judge that begged it, and indeed
Deserved it too; and then the boy, his clerk,
That took some pains in writing, he begged mine,
And neither man nor master would take aught
But the two rings.

Portia.   What ring gave you, my lord?
Not that, I hope, which you received of me.

Bassanio. If I could add a lie unto a fault,
I would deny it; but you see my finger
Hath not the ring upon it, it is gone.

190 *Portia.* Even so void is your false heart of truth!
                                [*she turns away*
By heaven, I will ne'er come in your bed

Until I see the ring.

  Nerissa.   Nor I in yours,
Till I again see mine.

  Bassanio.   Sweet Portia,
If you did know to whom I gave the ring,
If you did know for whom I gave the ring,
And would conceive for what I gave the ring,
And how unwillingly I left the ring,
When naught would be accepted but the ring,
You would abate the strength of your displeasure.

  Portia. If you had known the virtue of the ring,   200
Or half her worthiness that gave the ring,
Or your own honour to contain the ring,
You would not then have parted with the ring..
What man is there so much unreasonable,
If you had pleased to have defended it
With any terms of zeal, wanted the modesty
To urge the thing held as a ceremony?
Nerissa teaches me what to believe—
I'll die for't but some woman had the ring.

  Bassanio. No, by my honour, madam, by my soul,   210
No woman had it, but a civil doctor,
Which did refuse three thousand ducats of me,
And begged the ring, the which I did deny him,
And suffered him to go displeased away,
Even he that had held up the very life
Of my dear friend....What should I say, sweet lady?
I was enforced to send it after him,
I was beset with shame and courtesy,
My honour would not let ingratitude
So much besmear it...Pardon me, good lady,   220
For by these blessèd candles of the night,
Had you been there, I think you would have begged
The ring of me to give the worthy doctor.

Portia. Let not that doctor e'er come near my house.
Since he hath got the jewel that I loved,
And that which you did swear to keep for me,
I will become as liberal as you,
I'll not deny him any thing I have,
No, not my body, nor my husband's bed:
230 Know him I shall, I am well sure of it.
Lie not a night from home. Watch me, like Argus.
If you do not, if I be left alone,
Now, by mine honour, which is yet mine own,
I'll have that doctor for my bedfellow.

Nerissa. And I his clerk; therefore be well advised
How you do leave me to mine own protection.

Gratiano. Well, do you so: let not me take him then,
For if I do, I'll mar the young clerk's pen.

Antonio. I am th'unhappy subject of these quarrels.

240 *Portia.* Sir, grieve not you—you are welcome
    notwithstanding.

Bassanio. Portia, forgive me this enforcéd wrong,
And in the hearing of these many friends
I swear to thee, even by thine own fair eyes
Wherein I see myself—

Portia.   Mark you but that!
In both my eyes he doubly sees himself:
In each eye, one. Swear by your double self,
And there's an oath of credit.

Bassanio.   Nay, but hear me....
Pardon this fault, and by my soul I swear,
I never more will break an oath with thee.

250 *Antonio.* I once did lend my body for his wealth,
Which but for him that had your husband's ring
Had quite miscarried. I dare be bound again,
My soul upon the forfeit, that your lord
Will never more break faith advisedly.

Portia. Then you shall be his surety....[*she takes a ring from her finger*] Give him this,
And bid him keep it better than the other.
  Antonio. Here, Lord Bassanio, swear to keep this ring.
  Bassanio. By heaven, it is the same I gave the doctor!
  Portia. I had it of him: pardon me, Bassanio,
For by this ring the doctor lay with me.   260
  Nerissa [*shows a ring also*]. And pardon me, my
    gentle Gratiano,
For that same scrubbéd boy, the doctor's clerk,
In lieu of this last night did lie with me.
  Gratiano. Why, this is like the mending of highways
In summer, where the ways are fair enough.
What! are we cuckolds ere we have deserved it?
  Portia. Speak not so grossly. You are all amazed:
Here is a letter, read it at your leisure—
It comes from Padua, from Bellario.
There you shall find that Portia was the doctor,   270
Nerissa there, her clerk. Lorenzo here
Shall witness I set forth as soon as you,
And even but now returned; I have not yet
Entered my house. Antonio, you are welcome,
And I have better news in store for you
Than you expect: unseal this letter soon,
There you shall find three of your argosies
Are richly come to harbour suddenly.
You shall not know by what strange accident
I chancéd on this letter.
  Antonio.   I am dumb!   280
  Bassanio. Were you the doctor, and I knew you not?
  Gratiano. Were you the clerk that is to make
    me cuckold?
  Nerissa. Ay, but the clerk that never means to do it,
Unless he live until he be a man.

Bassanio. Sweet doctor, you shall be my bedfellow—
When I am absent, then lie with my wife.
   Antonio. Sweet lady, you have given me life
     and living;
For here I read for certain that my ships
Are safely come to road.
   Portia. How now, Lorenzo?
290 My clerk hath some good comforts too for you.
   Nerissa. Ay, and I'll give them him without a fee.
There do I give to you and Jessica,
From the rich Jew, a special deed of gift,
After his death, of all he dies possessed of.
   Lorenzo. Fair ladies, you drop manna in the way
Of starvéd people.
   Portia. It is almost morning,
And yet I am sure you are not satisfied
Of these events at full. Let us go in,
And charge us there upon inter'gatories,
300 And we will answer all things faithfully.
   Gratiano. Let it be so. The first inter'gatory
That my Nerissa shall be sworn on is,
Whether till the next night she had rather stay,
Or go to bed now, being two hours to-day:
But were the day come, I should wish it dark,
Till I were couching with the doctor's clerk.
Well, while I live I'll fear no other thing
So sore as keeping safe Nerissa's ring. *[they all go in*

THE COPY FOR
THE MERCHANT OF VENICE, 1600

A. *The Hayes Quarto* (1600), *the Jaggard Quarto* (1619), *and the Folio text*

There are three primary texts for *The Merchant of Venice*: the Quarto 'printed by I. R. for Thomas Heyes...1600,' the Quarto 'printed by J. Roberts, 1600,' and the Folio version printed in 1623. The last-named need give us little trouble, since according to the long-standing verdict of scholars it was reprinted from a copy of the Hayes Quarto which had been used as a prompt-book in the theatre or, at the least, had been collated with such a prompt-book; and this verdict, as we shall find (v. pp. 173–77), is fully borne out by a bibliographical comparison of the texts concerned. On the other hand, until about twelve years ago, critics were unable to agree upon the relative authority of the two quartos. Thus, the 'Cambridge' editors of 1863 preferred the 'Roberts' [i.e. Jaggard] Quarto on the ground that it 'seems to have been printed by a more accurate printer or overseen by a more accurate corrector' than the Hayes Quarto, while Dr Furnivall stoutly maintained with Johnson and Capell that the Hayes Quarto was the better of the two[1]. Furnivall appears, however, to have believed with Clark and Wright that the two books were independently printed from the same MS, or from different copies of the same MS, and that the 'Roberts' Quarto, though belonging to the same year, was the earlier edition of the play.

As against all this, modern bibliography has now proved that the Hayes Quarto was not merely earlier than the 'Roberts' Quarto but nineteen years earlier, and further that the 'Roberts' Quarto was not printed

[1] v. Forewords to Griggs Facsimile of 'Roberts' Quarto.

by Roberts at all but by Jaggard, who took over his business about 1608, and was later responsible for the First Folio. Nor is this the end of the story, for the 'Roberts' Quarto of *The Merchant of Venice* was only one of a set of ten plays, all by or attributed to Shakespeare, and all printed in 1619 by Jaggard, who three years after Shakespeare's death evidently thought it good business to issue a volume with some pretensions to being a collected edition of the dramatist. The nature of these pretensions may be gathered from the names of the plays which appeared in this curious medley. They are: *The Whole Contention* (2 pts), *Pericles*, *A Yorkshire Tragedy*, *Sir John Oldcastle*, *Henry V*, *The Merchant of Venice*, *A Midsummer-Night's Dream*, *King Lear*, *The Merry Wives of Windsor*. These were, of course, all reprints, four from Quartos wrongly attributed to Shakespeare, three from Bad Shakespearian Quartos, and another three from Good Quartos. For the thrilling story of the stages in this remarkable discovery—how Mr A. W. Pollard's suspicions were first aroused by two separate volumes of these Quartos coming under his eyes at an interval of three or four years; how Mr W. W. Greg then came forward and showed from the evidence of watermarks, the similarity of imprints and devices, and the common use of certain large numerals, that all ten plays must have been printed together in 1619; how Mr A. W. Pollard in his turn followed this up by establishing the typographical identity of the volume with Jaggard's acknowledged work; and how an American scholar, Mr William Neidig, furnished the final and irrefutable proof by demonstrating through photography that the same typographical setting had been used for seven out of the nine title-pages—for all this, we say, the reader must be referred to Mr A. W. Pollard's own account in his *Shakespeare Folios and Quartos*, 1909[1].

[1] Ch. iii. Other accounts may be found in *Shakespeare's*

In the course of this account, Mr Pollard incidentally points out that so far from the Jaggard *Merchant of Venice* (1619) being independently printed from the same manuscript as the Hayes Quarto, as the 'Cambridge' editors had believed, it was set up from the Hayes Quarto itself. Nevertheless, as we shall find (cf. pp. 173–77), the surmise of the 'Cambridge' editors was not entirely without justification, seeing that the Jaggard Quarto contains variants which cannot be explained as ordinary printing-house vagaries but must be accounted for by some kind of editorial interference with the text. It seems possible that this editor, whoever he may have been, had some connexion with the theatre. But of one thing at any rate we can feel certain, namely that his 'corrections' possess no Shakespearian authority whatsoever. The only text of this play which can command the respect of a modern editor is the Hayes Quarto of 1600.

B. *The publication and printing of the Hayes Quarto*

The first appearance of *The Merchant of Venice* in print was heralded by two separate entries in the Stationers' Register, which run as follows:

1598] xxij° Julij. James Robertes. Entred for his copie vnder the handes of bothe the wardens, a booke of the Marchant of Venyce, or otherwise called the Jewe of Venyce, Prouided, that yt bee not prynted by the said James Robertes or anye other whatsoeuer without lycence first had from the Right honorable the lord chamberlen. vj^d.

1600] 28 octobris. Thomas haies. Entred for his copie under the handes of the Wardens and by Consent of master Robertes. A booke called the booke of the merchant of Venyce vj^d.

The first of these has been explained by Mr Pollard as

Fight with the Pirates (2nd edition), and *The Bibliographical Study of Shakespeare*, by Percy Simpson (Oxford Bib. Soc. I. i).

a 'staying' entry, made in the interest of the Lord
Chamberlain's Men in order to prevent piracy, Roberts
as holder of a privilege for printing all play-bills being
an appropriate agent for the players[1]. Two years later,
as the 'I. R.' of the Q. title-page shows, he was allowed
to print the book as a reward.

Of Thomas Hayes the publisher little need be said.
His first book-entry was made in the same year as his publication of *The Merchant* and his last in September, 1602,
shortly after which he died. Roberts the printer is a far
more interesting person, whom we shall come across again
more than once in later volumes of this edition. He
printed a quarto of *Titus Andronicus* in 1600 together
with the 1604–5 text of *Hamlet*, and he made a 'con-
ditional entry' of *Troilus and Cressida* in 1603, though
he was not concerned with its publication in 1609. He
acquired the privilege to print all play-bills, noted above,
from John Charlewood, whose widow he married in
1593, thereby coming into the possession of numerous
copyrights and a printing-house 'well furnished with
type blocks and devices[2].' This being so, it is somewhat
remarkable to find him short of type in the printing of
The Merchant of Venice. Somewhere about 1608 he
sold his business to William Jaggard, who made free
with his name, as we have seen, in his 'Shakespearian'
volume of 1619.

Roberts' printing of the quarto is, on the whole, a
competent piece of work, but it would have been better
had he not, for some reason, starved his compositors of
type. So short, indeed, were they of roman capitals
that quite a large proportion of the verse-lines begin
with lower-case letters. And the poverty of capitals
appears to have affected the italic as well as the roman

---

[1] *Shakespeare Folios and Quartos*, pp. 66–67; *Shakespeare's Fight*, pp. xii–xiv.

[2] McKerrow, *Dictionary of Printers and Booksellers
1557–1640*. Bib. Soc. Pub.

founts. At least that seems to us a possible explanation of the otherwise apparently meaningless variation of *Shy.* and *Iew.* as speech-headings for Shylock[1]. There is little to suggest that this variation derives from the 'copy' as similar variations have seemed to do in other texts, while *S* is certainly a hard-worked letter in the prefixes of this play, not only because Shylock has much to say but also because Solanio and Salerio have to be provided for. Another italic capital much in evidence in certain scenes is *L*, which was needed for Lorenzo and Lancelot, who often appear together; and this perhaps helps to account for the frequent, though by no means universal, prefix of *Clowne* to Lancelot's speeches[2]. Finally, the text contains a surprising number of question-marks, many of them clearly incorrect, a feature which would be easily explained on the supposition that the compositors were short of colons and occasionally ran out of periods, and so had to make shift with notes of interrogation. Apart from this, however, the pointing of the quarto is good, better indeed than anything of the kind we have seen since we left the Folio texts and entered the batch of Quartos of which the present play is the last. It has not the brilliance of notation in *The Tempest*, but it can hardly be doubted that the punctuation of the 'copy' derived ultimately from the playhouse, though scarcely from the author himself. It is possible too that this distinction which seems to mark out *The Merchant*, 1600, from the other three quartos already edited and to link it on to the Folio texts, may be allied to features we have now to consider, which seem to point in the same direction.

[1] An instance of the same kind of thing, which can with certainty be thus explained, occurs in the Jaggard *M.N.D.*, v. p. 154 *M.N.D.* in this edition.

[2] It is of course conceivable that some or all of these variations were due to the revision which has left its marks elsewhere in the text.

C. *The nature of the Copy*

In considering the quartos of *Much Ado, Love's Labour's Lost* and *A Midsummer-Night's Dream* we found good reason for supposing that the printers of those texts had been furnished with manuscript prompt-books, which bore clear traces of revision and were evidently very much in the condition in which Shakespeare finally handed them over to his company's book-holder or prompter for the making out of players' parts and the drawing up of the theatrical plots. It needs but a casual glance through the Hayes Quarto of *The Merchant* to see that the copy used by James Roberts in 1600 was of a very different character.

In the first place we have to notice certain remarkable features connected with the 'letters' read aloud in 3. 2. and 4. 1., and with the three 'scrolls' belonging to the casket-scenes. The first of these letters, together with Portia's request to Bassanio that she may hear it and her subsequent comment, is thus printed in the Quarto:

But let me heare the letter of your friend.

Sweet Bassanio, *my ships haue all miscaried, my Creditors growe cruell, my estate is very low, my bond to the Iewe is forfaite, and since in paying it, it is impossible I should liue, all debts are cleerd betweene you and I if I might but see you at my death: notwithstanding, vse your pleasure, if your loue do not perswade you to come, let not my letter.*

Por. O loue! dispatch all busines and be gone.

Save that it is in roman and not italic type, Bellario's letter in 4. 1. is printed in exactly similar fashion; that is to say, it is unassigned to any speaker, is marked off from the surrounding context by spaces, and occurs between two speeches belonging to the same character (in this case the Duke), the second of which has a fresh prefix. Editors have, of course, found no difficulty in assigning the letter in 3. 2. to Bassanio; but Capell, evidently puzzled by the second *Duke* prefix, invented a 'Clerk' to read the letter in 4. 1., and most editors have followed suit. Yet there is no dramatic reason why the Duke should not himself read the letter aloud to the court, and strong theatrical reasons against increasing the number of speaking parts by giving the task to a 'clerk.' We have, therefore, removed the second *Duke* prefix, and thus made the letter part of the Duke's speech. And we do so with the less hesitation, that this is exactly the change which all editors have been compelled to make in regard to the three 'scrolls' of the casket-scenes. Each of these 'scrolls' is preceded and followed by lines belonging to the suitor who reads the 'scroll' aloud, and the lines that follow are in all cases marked off in the Quarto by a new speech-heading[1], which the editors have of course omitted.

Quite apart from questions of true reading, we have here a textual fact of capital importance. For the absence of prefixes before the letters and the duplication of prefixes in the speeches afford clear evidence that both letters and scrolls are, bibliographically speaking, textually distinct from the rest of the copy, or in other words, insertions. Nor is it at all difficult to imagine how they came to be so. From the actor's point of view 'lines' may be divided into two categories: those which have to be learnt by heart, and those which are to be read aloud from the stage or sung to music. And it is obvious that the second class, which includes stage-letters, songs, inscriptions, epitaphs and scrolls of all kinds, would not be transcribed into the players' parts, but would be written out on special pieces of paper for use on the stage itself. Of course a dramatist, in composing or revising a play, would not be at all likely to

---

[1] In the case of Bassanio, whose 'scroll' comes at the foot of a page, the second prefix occurs in the catch-word, but was omitted from the first line of the following page, possibly because the compositor noticed that it was unnecessary. Its occurrence in the catch-word, however, proves that it was present in the copy.

distinguish such portions of his manuscript from the rest. Nor, as a matter of fact, do we find them so distinguished in the quartos hitherto reviewed in this edition. *Love's Labour's Lost*, for instance, is full of 'sonnets' and 'letters' to be read aloud, and these were indubitably an integral part of the author's manuscript, since they are headed with appropriate prefixes or even sometimes with special stage-directions. Similarly the songs in *A Midsummer-Night's Dream* are textually so inseparable from the dialogue, that it is sometimes difficult for a modern editor to tell what is song and what is speech. It was only when the author had done his work and passed his manuscript over to the book-holder for re-hearsal and the making out of 'parts' for the actors, that a differentiation of the stage-papers from the rest of the dialogue would take place. Any text, therefore, in which letters, songs or scrolls are seemingly insertions, is to be suspected of being derived, not from the original 'book,' but from some secondary theatrical source, composed of players' parts[1]. And, as it happens, the two Folio texts in which we have already met these textually detached stage-papers, namely *The Two Gentlemen* (v. note 3. 1. 140) and *Measure for Measure* (v. note 4. 2. 119–25), are texts which on other grounds we have suspected of this secondary origin. The theory works well enough as regards the letters and the scrolls in *The Merchant*; but what about the song, 'Tell me where is Fancy bred'? If we turn to this song in the Quarto, we find nothing remarkable about it except that it is prefaced by an unusually elaborate stage-direction: 'A Song the whilst Baffanio comments on the caskets to himfelfe.' It is just the kind of description

---

[1] The only Elizabethan 'part' that has come down to us, that of Orlando in Greene's *Orlando Furioso*, omits the roundelays which Orlando was to read from papers hung up on the stage. For important deductions from the fact v. W. W. Greg, *Alcazar and Orlando*, pp. 302–3, 350–51.

which causes a certain type of critic to invoke some shadowy 'literary editor' to explain it. No such invocation is necessary here, however. For the song, like the scrolls and the letters, would certainly be copied out from the prompt-book on to a separate piece of paper; the paper, not in this case kept by the book-holder with the parts, but handed out to the musicians for practice, would naturally require some sort of title, to distinguish it from other songs in the musicians' repertory; and the descriptive heading in the Quarto is just the sort of title which might be written upon it. Everything, in short, seems to indicate that the Quarto of *The Merchant of Venice* was printed from some kind of assembled text made up of players' parts, into which the stage-papers had been fitted in somewhat amateurish fashion.

This conclusion appears to find support in the character of the stage-directions, to which we must now turn. It is a remarkable fact that, save for exits and entries, there are only two brief stage-directions in the whole of the Quarto. Indeed, were it not that some of the entries are rather elaborate in style, the text would seem almost as bare as those of *The Two Gentlemen* and *The Merry Wives*. Furthermore, these entry-directions have obviously not been taken from the same source as the dialogue. An interesting illustration of this is to be seen in the spelling of Lancelot's surname, which is 'Gobbo' in the stage-direction (2. 2. 29) and all subsequent speech-headings, but is six times given as 'Iobbe' in Lancelot's speech at the opening of the scene (2. 2. 3–8), the only occasion on which it appears in the dialogue. The name should, we think, be 'Giobbe,' the Italian form of our English 'Job' (cf. note 2. 2. 3–8); but the point we wish to make here is that, while the word in the dialogue represents the right sound, that of the stage-direction seems to be a 'correction' of the original by someone not unacquainted with

Italian[1]. Another clue pointing towards the same diver-
gence of origin is the frequent vagueness of the entry-
directions as compared with the dialogue. Thus at 2.2.109
we have 'Enter Baffanio with a follower or two,' but in
l. 167 we find Bassanio addressing one of these followers as 'Leonardo,' who replies in speeches headed
'Leon.' Similarly the 'man of Portias' who appears in
the entry at the head of 3. 4. turns out in ll. 45, 56 to
be 'Balthazar,' while the 'Meffenger' who enters at
5. 1. 24 is discovered four lines later to be Stephano,
one of Portia's household. The only text in which we
have come across this kind of thing before is *The Comedy
of Errors*, 1623, and the explanation which seemed to
fit the facts there was that the dialogue had been copied
out (from the players' parts) by one scribe and the
stage-directions supplied by another, who 'possessed
very vague ideas of the text he was working on' (v.
Errors, pp. 68–74). Are we to attribute the anomalies
in the transmitted text of *The Merchant* to a similar
cause? It looks like it.

Only ignorance of the play on the part of the scribe
responsible for the stage-directions will, we feel, account
for what may conveniently, if a little irreverently, be
called the muddle of the three Sallies. Most modern
editors give the names Salanio, Salarino and Salerio in
their lists of *dramatis personae*. The first of these names
appears as 'Solanio' (or its abbreviations) everywhere
in the Hayes Quarto except in the entries at the head of
1. 1. and 2. 4. and in one speech-heading (1. 1. 15);
and this would undoubtedly have been recognised as
the true form had not most editors hitherto believed the

---

[1] Gobbo, of course, means 'hunch-back,' an epithet
which is pointless as applied either to Lancelot or his father.
Elze traced in it a reference to the Gobbo di Rialto in
Venice 'a stone figure which serves as a supporter to the
granite pillar of about a man's height, from which the laws
of the Republic were proclaimed.'

Jaggard Quarto, which reads 'Salanio' throughout, to be the *editio princeps*. The mere fact, indeed, that abbreviations like 'Sol,' 'Sal,' 'Sola,' 'Sala' are frequently employed in the Hayes Quarto for the speeches of the two gentlemen proves that 'Solanio' is the correct spelling, for such abbreviations would be impossible if the two names began with the same four letters, as we can see from the Jaggard text which is forced to resort to 'Salan' and 'Salar' in the speech-headings. Nevertheless the three instances of 'Salanio' in the Hayes Quarto, two of them occurring at the very opening of the play, undoubtedly gave a wrong lead to the editor or the compositors of the 1619 edition and so caused all the trouble that followed. These three instances may, of course, be misprints. We are more inclined, however, to attribute them to a scribe who drafted the stage-directions, seeing that this scribe was almost certainly responsible for the form of the second name, 'Salarino.'

'Salarino' and 'Solanio' appear together in 1. 1., 2. 4., 2. 8., and 3. 1., while 'Salerino' enters with Gratiano in 2. 6. After 3. 1., however, we hear nothing more of them, at least in the Hayes Quarto, and their place is taken by 'Salerio.' Now this 'Salerio,' the third of our Sallies, is a remarkable fellow, whose appearance has raised suspicions in more than one editorial breast. He comes on first towards the end of Bassanio's casket-scene at Belmont (3. 2. 218), and his entry is thus printed in the 1600 Quarto:

Gra. No, we ſhall nere win at that ſport and ſtake downe.
But who comes here? *Lorenzo* and his infidell?
what, and my old Venecian friend *Salerio?*

   Enter *Lorenzo, Ieſſica,* and *Salerio* a meſſenger
       from Venice.
Baſſa. Lorenzo and *Salerio,* welcome hether

The scene that immediately follows transports us from Belmont to Venice and shows us Antonio, accom-

panied by a gaoler and a friend, in conversation with
Shylock. Yet here, strangely enough, the name 'Salerio'
figures once again as that of the friend in the stage-
direction of the Hayes Quarto, although as the 'Cambridge' editors remark, he 'cannot be the same person
as the messenger to Belmont.' This indeed was seen as
early as 1619, for the Jaggard Quarto has altered the
'Salerio' to 'Salarino,' while the Folio text of four
years later reads 'Solanio.' Most modern editions follow
the 1619 Quarto in this respect, and one or two have
even ventured to get rid of 'Salerio' altogether by putting
'Salanio' or 'Solanio' in his place in 3. 2. Knight, for
example, who reads 'Solanio' in 3. 2., believed 'Salerio'
to be a simple misprint, and points out that one whom
Gratiano addresses as 'my old Venetian friend' is far
more likely to have been 'Solanio' or 'Salarino' than a
new character of thom we have previously heard
nothing. Moreover, as he acutely observes, in 3. 1.
Solanio and Salarino are summoned to the house of the
unfortunate Antonio, and 'what can be more natural
than that, after the conference, the one should be
dispatched to Bassanio, and the other remain with him,
whose "creditors grow cruel"?' Knight's premisses are
very strong; why then have editors hesitated to adopt
the alteration which seems to be required by them?
Partly, because while the Hayes Quarto alone reads
'Salerio' in 3. 3., this name is given by all three primary
texts in 3. 2., and partly, we think, because (i) the
vague description, 'a messenger from Venice,' in the
entry at 3. 2. 218, seems ill-suited to a character we have
met with before, and (ii) the name 'Salerio' occurs
no less than four times in the dialogue of 3. 2., and
critics have rightly been chary of changing a name thus
buttressed by authority.

The truth is that Knight was correct in his premisses,
but wrong in his conclusions. For the following con-
siderations should show that 'Salerio' must be the true

form and 'Salarino' merely a corruption of it. In the first place, 'Salerio' is the only one of the three names under consideration to appear in the dialogue of the play; 'Solanio' and 'Salarino' are mere cast-names which are never uttered on the stage and occur in the stage-directions and prefixes alone. 'Salerio' is therefore in a very strong position indeed from the textual point of view. In the second place, the presence of 'Sol' as a prefix at 3. 3. 18 is good evidence that the gentleman who accompanied Antonio and the gaoler to the house of Shylock in that scene was, as the Folio reads, 'Solanio' and not, as Jaggard and most modern editions read, 'Salarino.' It follows from this that the 'Salerio' who visits Belmont in 3. 2. cannot be, as Knight supposed, identical with 'Solanio.' On the other hand, we get a kind of textual link between the names 'Salerio' and 'Salarino' in the form 'Salerino' which occurs among the entries at the head of 2. 6. and in the prefix 'Saleri' which unexpectedly crops up at 3. 1. 70. We can feel pretty certain then that 'Salerio' and 'Salarino' refer to the same character, and that the second is simply a corruption of the first. The fact that it is a syllable too long for the metre on the four occasions on which the dialogue gives us 'Salerio' should be sufficient in itself to show which is the true form.

Whence then came this curious 'Salarino'? If we assume, as we have already found ourselves entitled to assume, that the text before us was made up of players' parts strung together, transcribed and then worked over by a scribe who supplied the stage-directions, the reply is not difficult. Like his counterpart in *The Comedy of Errors*[1], whom we called Hand B, this scribe had before him at the outset, we must suppose, a transcript from the

[1] The curious spelling 'in' (=e'en) which occurs in *Errors* 2. 2. 101 and *Merchant* 3. 5. 20 suggests that the transcripts from the players' parts may have been made by the same scribe in both cases.

parts containing only the bare dialogue and the abbreviated prefixes, so that he would be obliged to rely
upon his memory of the play upon the stage for the full
names of those characters which were not mentioned
in the dialogue itself. Now the form 'Salarino' is found,
apart from the stage-directions, nowhere in the dialogue
and in only one prefix, which occurs at 1. 1. 8. The
prefix 'Salari' (which is of course a variant spelling of
'Saleri') is, on the other hand, fairly frequent. The
beginning of all the muddle, we suggest, was that the
scribe found the prefix 'Salari' in his text at 1. 1. 8,
took it as a contraction for 'Salarino,' added 'no' to it,
and framed his entry-direction accordingly. It accords
with this theory that the only time we get the erroneous
'Salanio' in the prefixes is at 1. 1. 15, that is to say also
the first page of the Quarto. Clearly, we think, the
meddling scribe made the two changes at the same time.
At any rate, 'Salarino' (or 'Salerino') marches happily
along in the stage-directions hand in hand with 'Salanio'
(or 'Solanio') up to the end of 3. 1., by which time the
former name had become such a habit with the scribe
that when he comes upon 'Salerio' in the dialogue of
3. 2. he quite fails to recognise his identity and puts
him down as 'a messenger from Venice.' Nevertheless,
the four references to 'Salerio' in 3. 2. seem to have
left their impression, for when he passes to the next
scene and finds 'Sol' as a prefix, he takes it to be
'Salerio' once again. And even so he has not quite
finished with him, since we have a 'Salerio' acting as
a kind of door-keeper to the Duke's court in 4. 1.,
although no entry is provided for him. The Salarino-
Salerio business, in short, is a close parallel with that of
Antipholis-Antipholus in *Errors* (v. pp. 73–4).

And there is yet another point in which these texts
are alike: the stage-directions in either were written not
for publication but for performance. This is particularly
important in the present instance as precluding the

possibility of a special text having been made up for Roberts in 1598 (cf. p. 94). In other words *The Merchant*, 1600, was printed from a sort of prompt-book, though not from the original prompt-book. Our reasons for thinking this to be so are few, but we hope sufficient. We noted, it will be remembered, that the text possessed only two stage-directions apart from the entries and exits. These are 'open the letter' (3. 2. 237) and 'play Muſique' (5. 1. 69); and both, couched as they are in the imperative mood, are indubitably theatrical in origin, as indeed is 'Ieſſica aboue,' the entry found at 2. 6. 25. Another clue pointing in the same direction is the curious heading to 2. 5., 'Enter Iewe and his man that was the Clowne.' Clearly, we think, this heading, after the vague manner of the scribe concerned, originally ran 'Enter Iewe and his man that was,' referring, of course, to Lancelot who has just exchanged Shylock's service for Bassanio's. Such a description, however, was too obscure for stage-purposes, and accordingly the words 'the Clowne' have been added as a marginal clarification, possibly at the time of rehearsal.

Lastly, texts derived from secondary theatrical manu-scripts are likely to preserve traces of actors', or at least of playhouse, additions, and such traces as we have found, for example, in *The Two Gentlemen* and *Measure for Measure*, affect comic or fantastic parts, the clowns as ever being prone to speak 'more than is set down for them' in the original prompt-book. It is, therefore, a significant fact, which offers a considerable support to our main theory, that a piece of 'fat,' as the modern actor would call it, has quite clearly been inserted in the text of *The Merchant* at the beginning of 5. 1. in order to provide an additional entry for Lancelot. Act 5, which contains of course only one scene, consists wholly of verse, except for eleven lines of prose (ll. 39–49) which are concerned with Lancelot's entry 'sola'-ing like a 'post' to announce Bassanio's approach. Lancelot is a clown and speaks prose throughout the play; otherwise this prose-patch in the midst of verse might raise suspicions of itself. There is, however, another point about the passage which unmistakably indicates textual irregularity, and demands explanation: the words 'sweet soul,' which should of course stand in l. 50 at the beginning of Lorenzo's speech, have been misplaced and are printed by Q. in l. 49 at the end of Lancelot's speech. So that the text runs thus in Q.:

Clow. Tell him there's a Poſt come from my Maiſter, with his horne full of good newes, my Maiſter will be heere ere morning ſweete ſoule.

Loren. Let's in, and there expect their comming.

Suspecting this irregularity to be a clue of importance and fearful lest his own bias in favour of an assembled text might influence his interpretation of it, the textual editor determined to submit the point to the judgment of an independent scholar. Accordingly, without giving him any inkling of what he had in mind, he consulted Dr W. W. Greg, whose authority on matters of this kind is unrivalled and to whose generous assistance this edition is already very deeply indebted. The question put was, 'How would you explain the misplacement of "sweet soul" at 5. 1. 49?'; and the reply ran as follows: 'I think it is pretty clear that the preceding passage was an insertion in the margin, or more probably on a slip, ending up, as was usual, with a repetition of the *following* words to show where it was to come. The sense shows that the insertion must have begun with the Messenger's words: "I pray you is my Maister yet returnd?" I suppose that the printer finding the words repeated in the MS, omitted the second occurrence. The compositor would not be very likely to do this, but a proof-reader might—or there may have been an intermediate transcript.' It will, of course, be noticed that the passage, as defined by Dr Greg, might be

omitted without any injury to the context, seeing that
(i) Lorenzo's 'Sweet soul, let's in, and there expect
their coming' follows perfectly naturally upon the
Messenger's 'None, but a holy hermit and her maid,'
and (ii) there is no dramatic necessity for Bassanio's
advent to be announced at this point; Lorenzo's an-
nouncement at l. 123 is quite adequate for the
purpose. It will be noticed too how aptly Dr Greg's
explanation of the puzzle falls in with our general
theory of the copy as outlined above, even to the hint
of 'an intermediate transcript.' But why was the insertion made? There can be only one answer: to give
the clown who played Lancelot an opportunity of
making the theatre ring with his 'sola!' The whole
business, stupid as it seems to us, is closely paralleled,
as it happens, in the 'so-ho'-ing of Launce at 3. 1. 189
of *The Two Gentlemen*; evidently the clown in Shakespeare's company, Will Kempe presumably, was fond of
caterwauling tricks[1].

And if an addition was made to this 'assembled'
prompt-book at one place, why not at others? There is
another prose-patch, this time of a ribald nature, to be
found in the verse-texture of 3. 2. (v. note ll. 214–18),
and once again it may be omitted without injury to the
context. It is pretty certainly a textual addition, and we
suspect that it was made by the same hand as wrote the
'sola' slip. Indeed, we are inclined to go even further and
to attribute a whole scene to this unknown scribe. There
is a passage in 3. 5. sufficiently described by Furness as
'Lorenzo's unpleasant banter with Lancelot,' which the
same editor believed to be 'an outcropping of the old
play' over which Shakespeare worked (v. note 3. 5. 34–9).
It concerns a black woman, to whom no reference is
made elsewhere in the text, and is therefore probably a
topical allusion of some kind. Here, however, there is
no question of a prose-patch, seeing that the first 59

---

[1] Cf. the bawling of Jessica's name at 2. 5. 6.

lines of the scene are in prose, and it is clear that the passage about the black woman is of a piece with the rest. But it is the verse with which the scene closes that seems to provide the clue we are seeking. The first five and a half lines of this verse are a tribute to Lancelot, or rather to the actor who played him, while the reference to 'A many fools that stand in better place' is obviously intended as a hit at some successful rival. In a word, we suggest that Shakespeare had no hand whatever in the composition of 3. 5., which might be omitted altogether without loss to the play; that it was added to the 'assembled' prompt-book at the same time as the insertions at 5. 1. 39–49 and 3. 2. 214–18; and that while 3. 5. 60–5 was written by some second-rate poet as a compliment to William Kempe, Kempe himself may have been responsible for the very dull fifty-nine lines of prose with which the scene opens.

To sum up, our contention is that the manuscript used as copy by Roberts' compositors in 1600 contained not a line of Shakespeare's handwriting, but was some kind of prompt-book made up from players' parts, to which a theatrical scribe (maybe Kempe himself) had added stage-directions and additions of his own devising. In dealing with the transmitted text, we are therefore at least two, and probably three, removes from Shakespeare's original manuscript, a state of affairs very different from that in which we found ourselves in discussing the copy for *The Dream*, *Love's Labour's Lost*, and *Much Ado*. Nevertheless, it is not altogether impossible to discover something of the history and condition of the original manuscript, though the explorer must proceed with circumspection.

D. *The original manuscript*

The Quarto of 1600 contains a plentiful supply of those peculiarities which in previous texts we have taken as evidence of revision. There are, for example, broken lines, which when they occur in the middle of a speech and have no obvious dramatic or metrical significance are best explained as due to abridgment. Textual 'cuts,' however, especially in a text of this kind, need not necessarily denote author's revision; they may have been made by the book-holder to remove an obscurity, shorten a 'part' or abridge the length of a performance; or again they may be due to the adapter responsible for the playhouse transcript. It is only when they appear to be connected with partially suppressed elements of the plot that we can feel safe in regarding them as connected with revision proper. The opening lines of the Quarto, as it happens, provide an excellent instance of the kind of thing we mean:

In footh I know not why I am fo fad,
It wearies me, you fay it wearies you;
But how I caught it, found it, or came by it,
What ftuffe tis made of, whereof it is borne,
I am to learne: and fuch a want-wit fadnes makes of mee,
That I haue much adoe to know my felfe.

Antonio's sadness, which is never explained in the play as we have it, has given rise to much speculation among critics. Yet when all the references to it have been brought together, the cause is not difficult to trace, though from the acting point of view the matter is and was obviously intended to be obscure. In other words, as we take it, we have here a dramatic motive deliberately suppressed at the time of a revision, and the broken line 'I am to learne' shows us where one of the 'cuts' involved in this suppression took place[1]. It is worth noting in passing that the broken line here, like broken lines elsewhere in the text, does not stand alone, but has been printed with the following line, an arrangement which strongly suggests that the 'cut' was effected

[1] Cf. notes 1. 1. 1, 46, 145; 2. 8. 46–50; 3. 4. 2–3 for further observations on the point.

at some stage before the transcript, from which the Quarto was printed, was made.

An element of a different kind, which also appears to have been cut out or at least very much whittled down in revision, is the masquing at Bassanio's house on the eve of his departure for Belmont. No less than five consecutive scenes, including those concerned with the elopement of Jessica, lead up to this masque, which in the received text does not take place. In the first of them (2. 2.) there are three casual references to a supper which Bassanio is preparing for his friends, some of whom, we are told, 'purpose merriment.' Bibliographically, the scene bears all the marks of drastic revision. The first 139 lines, most of which are taken up with the fooling of the two Gobbos, are in prose, including speeches by Bassanio; but in ll. 143–203, which bring the scene to an end, Bassanio speaks only verse, though Lancelot talks prose and Gratiano a mixture of both. In this section, moreover, there crops up 'Leonardo,' one of those mysterious, unexplained characters whose presence in a Shakespearian text is an almost certain sign of revision. The scene that follows (2. 3.) gives us a brief conversation between Jessica and Lancelot in which she entrusts him with a letter to be delivered to Lorenzo at the supper, where he is to be Bassanio's guest. The scene is only twenty-one lines long, yet even here revision is evident. Jessica has two speeches in verse, Lancelot one in prose; and this prose speech is flanked by two broken lines of verse, so that it looks very much as if Lancelot once spoke verse likewise. In 2. 4. we find Gratiano, Lorenzo and others plotting to 'slink away in supper-time' in order to return disguised and surprise the party with an impromptu masque. It is a short scene, and the broken line 'Go, gentlemen' (l. 21) shows that it was once longer and probably contained more talk about the masque. Towards the end, we learn that Lorenzo intends Jessica in her page's suit to take part in this masque, and when in the following scene (2. 5.) we discover that Shylock has accepted Bassanio's invitation to supper (cf. 2. 4. 17–18), we are led to anticipate a pretty situation in which the Jew will unwittingly confront his disguised daughter in a Christian household. Our expectations, however, come surprisingly to nought in 2. 6., the scene of Jessica's elopement, at the end of which Antonio suddenly appears and puts a stop to all talk of supper and masque by announcing that 'the wind is come about' and that Bassanio is prepared to 'go aboard.' Now that this *dénouement* was an after-thought is suggested not merely by its abruptness, but also by the fact that Antonio's entry takes place immediately after the dismissal-couplet,

> What, art thou come? On, gentlemen, away—
> Our masquing mates by this time for us stay,

which brings the scene to a natural, almost an inevitable, close. In short, our belief is that *The Merchant of Venice* at one time contained a supper-scene at Bassanio's house, which at the entry of Gratiano, Lorenzo and the other disguised persons became one of those masque-scenes, of which we have other examples in *Much Ado, Romeo and Juliet, Love's Labour's Lost* and *Henry VIII,* and that this scene, being lengthy and not essential to the main plot, was thrown over in revision when room was needed for expansion elsewhere[1]. In any event, whether this hypothesis be sound or not, it is certain that there has been a considerable amount of textual alteration in the five scenes just considered. Nor do we think that anyone will seriously dispute that alteration of this kind, which is clearly concerned with questions of dramatic structure, should be attributed to Shakespeare himself.

Evidence which points in the same direction may be

[1] It was restored in the 18th century. v. p. 179.

found in other parts of the play. In 1. 1., for instance, we have a scene wholly in verse save for a curious little patch of six prose lines (ll. 113–18), in which Antonio and Bassanio comment upon the unseemly doggerel which Gratiano hurls at them as he goes off with Lorenzo. Significantly enough, this prose-patch, the language of which is in our view undoubtedly Shakespearian, occurs at the one point of the scene at which a complete break might be made, seeing that Gratiano's doggerel-couplet would form a natural scene-ending, while a fresh verse-scene altogether might as naturally begin with Antonio's 'Well, tell me now.' It looks in fact as if the conversation between the two friends about Portia originally formed a separate scene, which Shakespeare, for some purpose or other, possibly because he wished to delete an intermediate scene, found it convenient to tack on to 1. 1. when revising. At any rate, there is no doubt in our minds that the prose-patch denotes revision, and revision by Shakespeare of a play already drafted by himself; for if the prose be Shakespearian, the verse of 1. 1. is equally unmistakably his.

Are we to conclude, then, that *The Merchant of Venice* was an original dramatic creation by Shakespeare, which he revised at a later date? On the contrary, the general trend of critical opinion has insisted upon the probability that in this play, as in others, he was building upon the work of his predecessors. The two main plots, that concerning the bond and the pound of flesh and that in which the fate of courtiers hangs upon the choice of three caskets, are based on stories of immemorial antiquity; and it was for some time supposed that their combination in one dramatic structure was a stroke of Shakespeare's genius. Already in the eighteenth century, however, critics had discovered a passage in Gosson's *Schoole of Abuse* (1579) which speaks of *The Iew*, a play 'showne at the Bull' and 'representing the greedinesse of worldly chusers and bloody mindes of usurers'—words that, as nearly all have agreed, can only refer to pre-Shakespearian casket-scenes and a pre-Shakespearian Shylock. Grant White regarded the Bull prompt-book as the parent manuscript upon which Shakespeare later worked, and it is evident that Furness agreed with him. Furness even went so far as to declare 'it not unlikely that here and there, at two places at least, we may discern in the dialogue traces of the old play.' One of his 'two places,' the contradiction between the 'four' and the 'six' strangers at 1. 2. 118, seems possible enough; but for the other one, 'Lorenzo's unpleasant banter with Lancelot' in 3. 5., we have already accounted on other grounds. And though we strongly suspect the jingling 'scrolls' in the casket-scenes, the fragmentary scrap of doggerel at the end of 1. 2., and a good deal of the verse in 2. 2. and in some of the other abridged scenes, to be pre-Shakespearian matter, it is obvious that in a text like the present, which contains post-Shakespearian playhouse additions, mere surmise does not carry us very far. What we need is proof, and proof of such a kind as will leave no doubt that two distinct dramatists have been at work upon the structure of the play.

The divergent conceptions of the Venetian polity evident in the play, though hitherto unnoticed by critics, furnish, we think, the proof required. Consider these three passages:

> He plies the duke at morning and at night,
> And doth impeach the freedom of the state,
> If they deny him justice.   3. 2. 278–80.

> The duke cannot deny the course of law:
> For the commodity that strangers have
> With us in Venice, if it be denied,
> Will much impeach the justice of the state,
> Since that the trade and profit of the city
> Consisteth of all nations.   3. 3. 26–31.

> I have possessed your grace of what I purpose,
> And by our holy Sabbath have I sworn
> To have the due and forfeit of my bond.
> If you deny it, let the danger light
> Upon your charter and your city's freedom! 4. 1. 35–9.

In the second we recognise the historical Venetian Republic, the independent state, the great world-port and world-market, thronged with a host of foreign merchants, whose trade and confidence were only secured by the city's even-handed and rigorous enforcement of the law of contract. In the third passage the constitution has completely changed; Venice has now become a city, like London or many other English townships, enjoying privileges under a royal charter, privileges liable to suspension if the city misbehaved itself. As for the first of the three passages, it must remain uncertain what type of constitution it has in view, seeing that 'freedom' may refer either to 'the commodity [i.e. privileges] that strangers have' in the port of Venice, or to the freedom of the city itself from royal or baronial interference. Indeed one may hazard the guess that it was just the ambiguity of this word 'freedom' which gave rise to the contradiction in the other two passages. In any case, it can hardly be denied that the contradiction is there and that its presence makes it absolutely certain that two different dramatists had been at work upon the text. Nor, we think, should there be any hesitation in deciding which of the two was Shakespeare. The historically accurate lines from 3. 3. give us pedestrian and unskilful verse, witness the awkwardness of 'since that,' the ugly repetition in 'deny… denied,' and the muddled construction of the whole sentence which no commentator has quite succeeded in unravelling. On the other hand, the lines which inaccurately credit Venice with a royal charter come not only from the trial-scene but from the mouth of one of Shakespeare's supreme creations at his most characteristic moment. In revising the old prompt-book, we do not doubt, Shakespeare left the short scene 3. 3. very much as he found it, but borrowed therefrom (or from 3. 2.) the point about the danger to the state for use in the great court-scene, which of course he rewrote completely. And if in borrowing he converted the Venetian constitution into something which reminded his audience of their own London, who noticed or, if noticing, cared?

We can, therefore, feel tolerably sure that in creating his *Merchant of Venice* Shakespeare had an old play to go upon, which had some material connexion, probably through several intermediate handlings by various dramatists, with the prompt-book of *The Jew* which Gosson tells us was played at the Bull Inn in 1579. On the other hand, we have already found strong bibliographical evidence going to show that, after first of all revising this old play, Shakespeare, at some subsequent stage, revised his own revision. And this theory of a double Shakespearian revision falls in, it is satisfactory to note, with the general impressions set forth by Clark and Aldis Wright in their Clarendon edition. 'There are,' they write, 'in the play itself indications which would lead us to suppose that its first composition was earlier than 1598 [when Meres cites it in his list], such as the many classical allusions, the frequent rhymes and occasional doggerel verses. The fooling of Lancelot, too, has a strong resemblance to that of his almost namesake in *The Two Gentlemen of Verona*. On the other hand, the loftiness of thought and expression, the grace and freedom of versification in general, point to a later time, and would lead us rather to class this play with *Twelfth Night*, *As You Like It*, and *Much Ado About Nothing*, than with the earlier plays, *Love's Labour's Lost* and *The Two Gentlemen of Verona*. On the whole, we incline to think that the play was in part rewritten between the time of its first production in 1594 and its publication in 1600.'

The date 1594 which many critics subscribe to for the first Shakespearian production of the play was, we believe, originally advanced by Malone, who mainly founded it on an entry in Henslowe's *Diary* recording the performance on August 25th of that year of 'the Venesyon Comodey.' We know nothing of this 'comodey' except the name Henslowe gives it and that it belonged to the repertory of the Admiral's Men, a fact which makes any subsequent connexion with the Chamberlain's Men unlikely. Apart from this, however, it seems very probable that Shakespeare was re-creating *The Merchant* early in 1594, seeing that February, 1594, saw the beginning of the celebrated trial of the Jewish physician, Roderigo Lopez, on the charge of plotting the Queen's assassination together with that of Antonio the pretender to the Portuguese throne, a trial followed by his conviction, Elizabeth's reluctant signature of the death-warrant (she appears to have believed the man innocent), and the execution by hanging, drawing and quartering, amid universal execration, on June 7th at Tyburn. The attention of scholars was first drawn to these events by Sir Sidney Lee in an article entitled *The Original Shylock*, printed in 1880[1], which made out a plausible case on general grounds for a connexion between Lopez and Shylock. The trial and conviction of the Jewish doctor were due to the exertions of Essex, who owed him a grudge and who presided over the judicial proceedings at the Guildhall, like the Duke in the trial-scene, with the city fathers as his attendant magnificoes. The whole affair created a great deal of public excitement; and it is by no means certain that Lopez was guilty on either of the two charges laid against him. All things considered, it is

[1] In *The Gentleman's Magazine*, Feb. 1880; cf. also the article on Lopez in the *D.N.B.* and 'The conspiracy of Dr Lopez' by Rev. Arthur Dimock, *English Historical Review*, iv. 440 seq.

inconceivable that Shakespeare, the intimate of Southampton, himself the intimate of Essex, can have watched
these events without concern. And it is more than
likely that he began recasting the old *Jew* play in the
spring of 1594 when the trial of Lopez was the talk of
the town. In this connexion, it is significant to note
that Marlowe's *Jew of Malta* was performed at the
Rose on February 4th, 1594, and no less than fourteen
times later in the same year, though in 1595, when the
interest in Lopez had died down, no performances of
the play are recorded by Henslowe at all.

So much for Sir Sidney Lee's case in favour of
the Lopez-Shylock connexion. But it was left to
Dr Furness to detect a passage, which had escaped
Sir Sidney and to which even yet too little attention has
been given, although it appears to establish the fact of
a revision of the play in 1594 beyond all cavil. The
passage, which comes from one of Gratiano's railing
speeches in the trial-scene, runs thus:

> thy currish spirit
> Governed a Wolf, who hanged for human slaughter,
> Even from the gallows did his fell soul fleet,
> And whilst thou layest in thy unhallowed dam,
> Infused itself in thee.   4. 1. 133–37.

Furness notes (i) that though Gratiano speaks of 'a
Wolf,' he is evidently thinking of a man hanged for
murder, and (ii) that the allusion 'vague as it is, is quite
pointed enough to have been caught by an audience in
whose minds' the execution of the Jew at Tyburn was
still fresh; to which we may add (iii) that the allusion
was by no means so vague as Furness seems to have
thought, since 'Wolf' (the Q. capital is noteworthy) is
a kind of translated pun on the name Lopez![1] Furthermore, Furness, observing that 'the whole passage...can

---

[1] Lopez was popularly known as Doctor Lopus (cf.
Marlowe, *Doctor Faustus*, xi. 46) and from Lopus to Lupus
is no great step.

be omitted without injury either to the sense or to the rhythm,' was inclined to take it as an actor's interpolation. It may be so, though we cannot regard it as impossible verse for Shakespeare in a hurry, while the barbarity of the sentiment is quite in keeping with Gratiano's character. On the other hand, we agree that it was probably an addition, and if so then it must have been an addition made immediately after the execution of Lopez on June 7th, with a view to keeping up to date a play originally recast to make capital out of the public excitement at the trial. And if it be complained that this is to represent Shakespeare as one who deliberately set out to take advantage of, if not to gratify, the vulgar passions and prejudices of the mob, we reply (i) that he was a working dramatist, whose express intention was 'to hold, as 'twere, the mirror up to nature; to show virtue her own feature, scorn her own image, and the very age and body of the time his form and pressure'; (ii) that the Lopez affair was a matter of deep concern not merely to the populace but to all at court, and especially to the little circle of which his patron Southampton was a member; (iii) that modern Jews are by no means unanimous in interpreting the play as anti-Semitic in tendency; and (iv) that conceivably even (cf. note 4. 1. 181–99) Shakespeare, while faithfully mirroring in his play the passions aroused by the Lopez case, wrote it with the deliberate object of showing that even a Jew had human rights and deserved human mercy. Anyhow, there cannot, we think, be any reasonable doubt that the 'Wolf' passage was written in the summer of 1594, and that performances of *The Jew*, as revised by Shakespeare, were being given in the spring of that year. And if doubt still lingers in some minds it should yield to yet another topical reference, this time to the coronation of Henry IV of France on February 27th, 1594, which Malone discovered in 3. 2. 49–50 (v. note), and which must have been written shortly after the ceremony took place. It is not often that passages in the text of Shakespeare bring us as close to the calendar as these. We were, however, able to show reason for thinking that *Love's Labour's Lost*, in its first draft, was finished by Shakespeare in the autumn of 1593 for a performance at Christmas. It looks as though the first draft of *The Merchant of Venice* was the next thing he undertook after that. We have no suggestions to make as to the date or occasion of his second handling of the text; but we are none the less confident of its actuality.

[1926]   D. W.

P.S. (1952). A criticism of the foregoing provisional essay will be found in *William Shakespeare* by E. K. Chambers, 1930, i, pp. 369–75, and *The Editorial Problem in Shakespeare* by W. W. Greg, 1942, pp. 123–4. In 1926 the essential differences between prompt book and author's manuscript had not yet been defined. See note 1.1.27 for a clue to the date of the "second handling".

NOTES

All significant departures from the Quarto, including emendations in punctuation, are recorded; the name of the critic who first suggested a reading being placed in brackets. Illustrative spellings and misprints are quoted from the Good Quarto texts or from the Folio where no Good Quarto exists. The line-numeration for reference to plays not yet issued in this edition is that used in Bartlett's *Concordance*.

Q. stands for the Quarto of 1600 (Hayes); Q.1619 for the faked Jaggard Quarto, v. pp. 91–2; F., unless otherwise specified, for the First Folio; T.I. for the Textual Introduction to be found in the *Tempest* volume; Sh.Hand for *Shakespeare's Hand in the play of 'Sir Thomas More'* (Camb. Univ. Press, 1923); N.E.D. for *Oxford English Dictionary*; Sh.Eng. for *Shakespeare's England*; C.J.S. for C. J. Sisson; S.D. for Stage-direction; G. for Glossary.

Title-page of the Quarto. For 'I. R.' and 'Thomas Heyes' v. pp. 93–4. The running headline of the Quarto is 'The comicall History of the Merchant of Venice.'

Characters in the Play. Neither Q. nor F. gives a list, which first appeared on the back of the title-page of the Quarto issued in 1652 (cf. Pollard, *Census of Shak. Quartos*). Antonio is spelt 'Anthonio' throughout. For Solanio and Salerio cf. pp. 100–104; most modern edd. include a 'Salarino' in their lists. Shylock: the existence of a tract entitled 'A Iewes Prophesy' and containing a section headed 'Caleb Shilock his prophesie for the yeere 1607,' and of a ballad on the same matter called 'Calebbe Shillocke his Prophesie' shows that 'Shylock' was familiar, as a Jewish name, in England at this period, though of course the familiarity may be due to Shakespeare's play or its original. For Tubal,

v. Gen. **x**. 2. For 'Gobbo,' which we believe should rightly be 'Giobbe,' v. note 2. 2. 3–8.

Acts and Scenes. No divisions in Q. The F. divides into acts but not scenes.

Punctuation. On the whole, excellent, and (v. p. 95) at times beautiful. We have been able to follow it very closely, and to note every departure from the original in stops heavier than commas. Nearly all these departures concern full stops, which, we feel confident, were introduced somewhat freely into the text by the compositors.

Stage-directions. Cf. pp. 99–100, 104–105. All original S.D.s are given in the notes, according to Q., where Q. and F. are in substantial agreement; the Q. 1619 and F. S.D.s being also quoted where they differ from Q.

I. I.

S.D. Q. 'Enter Anthonio, Salaryno, and Salanio.' For 'Salaryno and Salanio' cf. pp. 100–104. The speech-headings for these characters run as follows in the scene: Salarino. (l. 8), Salanio. (l. 15), Salar. (l. 22), Sola. (ll. 46, 47, 57), Sala. (l. 60), Sal. (ll. 65, 68).

1. *I know not why I am so sad* This unexplained melancholy on the part of Antonio has been much commented upon by critics. Schücking (*Character Problems,* p. 171) suggests that Shakespeare inherited it from the original play upon which he worked. We think this likely, though, of course, the explanation may have been lost in Shakespeare's second rehandling of the text. In any event it is not difficult to guess at the root of Antonio's melancholy, when we put two and two together, a process which of course no dramatist should demand of us. It is clear from 1. 1. 73–6 that the distemper was of quite recent origin, while we also learn from 1. 1. 119–21 that Antonio had only just heard of Bassanio's attachment to a lady unknown. Is

not the secret of his melancholy the fear that this lady may rob him of his dear friend? Certainly the reported account of his farewell to Bassanio in 2. 8. (v. note 2. 8. 46–50) scarcely admits of any other interpretation, and we even seem to overhear the end of a conversation on the subject between Lorenzo and Portia at the opening of 3. 4. For the conflict between friendship and love, a favourite theme with Renaissance writers, see Herford, *Shakespeare's Treatment of Love and Marriage* (pp. 28–9), and of course the *Sonnets*.

5. *I am to learn* Printed with l. 6 in Q. This broken line, in the middle of a speech, is strongly suggestive of a 'cut.' Possibly the deleted matter would have thrown light upon the cause of Antonio's melancholy. Cf. p. 109.

13. *curtsy* 'Suggested by the rocking, ducking motion in the petty traffickers caused by the wake of the argosy as it sails past them' (Furness).

17. *abroad*. So Q.

18. *Plucking the grass* Johnson quotes from Ascham's *Toxophilus* 'I took a fether or a lytle light grasse, and so well as I could, learned how the wynd stood'—as modern people do with their pocket-handkerchiefs. Cf. Sh.Eng. ii. 381.

19. *Piring* (Q.) All edd. read 'peering' after 'piering' (Q. 1619). The Q. 'piring' which is not the same word as 'peering,' though closely allied to it in meaning (v. G.), avoids the jingle with 'piers.'

24. *sea*. So Q.

25. *hour-glass* Some have supposed that Shakespeare erred in making the nautical glass an hour and not a half-hour glass; but v. Sh.Eng. i. 164.

27. *Andrew*. A ship thus named was captured by Essex at Cadiz in 1596 and was much battered by storms in July 1597 (v. letter by E. Kuhl, *T.L.S.* 27. xii. 28) [1952].

docked (Rowe) Q. 'docks' Shakespeare probably wrote 'dockt', and the *t* may have been taken for a final *s*.

46. *Why then...fie* a short line. Hanmer made up
the missing syllables by reading 'Fie, fie, away!' Dyce
proposed 'In love! fie, fie!' But since 'Anth. o no'
might easily be read as 'Anthonio' perhaps what Shakespeare intended Antonio to say was 'O no! fie, fie!'
The expression 'fie,' which is nearly always connected
with strong disgust or contempt in Shakespeare, gives
us a clue to Antonio's attitude towards 'love'; cf. note
1. 1. 1.

50. *'sad.* So Q.

by two-headed Janus Cf. Greene, *Menaphon,* 1589
(ed. Arber, p. 23), 'The King thus smoothing the heate
of his cares, rested a melancholy man in his Courts;
hiding vnder his head the double faced figure of Janus,
as well to cleare the skies of other mens conceiptes with
smiles, as to furnish out his own dumps with thoughts.'

52. *peep* 'as in laughing, when the eyes are half
shut' (Warburton).

53. *laugh...bag-piper* i.e. scream with laughter at
the melancholy noise of the bagpipe. Cf. 1 *Hen. IV,*
1. 2. 83–7 'as melancholy as...the drone of a Lincoln-
shire bagpipe.' As Dowden points out, the true contrast
with the man of 'vinegar aspect' who will not smile
even at a genuine jest is the uproarious fellow who
shrieks with laughter at the most melancholy objects.

bag-piper; Q. 'bagpyper.'

54. *other* The old plural.

56. *Nestor* The type of wisdom and (here) of
gravity.

S.D. Q. 'Enter Baſſanio, Lorenſo, and Gratiano.'

57. *Here comes* etc. Q. heads this line with a new
prefix 'Sola.' Possibly the transcriber of the parts began
a fresh page here. Cf. note l. 112 below. All mod.
edd. follow Q. 1619 and assign the speech to 'Salan.'

62. *Your worth* etc. 'Antonio courteously protests
against his friend's self-disparagement' (Verity).

regard. So Q.

66. *when shall we laugh?* i.e. when is our next merry meeting to be?

68. S.D. Q. 'Exeunt Salarino, and Solanio.' Q. 1619 reads 'Salanio' for 'Solanio.'

72. *I will not fail you* broken line, but probably of no bibliographical significance. Q. 1619 inserts an erroneous 'Exit' here.

73–6. *You look not well* etc. Cf. note 1. 1. 1.

79. *play the fool* i.e. take the part of the stage-fool.

80. *With mirth...wrinkles come* Cf. *L.L.L.* 5. 2. 465 'That smiles his cheek in years.' The notion is that laughter as well as age may bring lines into the face.

82. *groans.* So Q.

84. *alabaster* Q. 'Alablaſter' N.E.D. explains this common 16–17th cent. spelling as 'apparently due to a confusion with "arblaster," a cross-bow man, also written "alablaster".'

87. *it is* (F.) Q. 'tis' *speaks—* Q. 'ſpeakes:'

88–99. *There are a sort of men* etc. This long description of Sir Oracle may perhaps be intended as a satirical allusion to some notability of the time: the portrait would suit the fellow of the 'vinegar aspect' to whom Solanio refers in ll. 54–6 above.

90. *a wilful stillness* i.e. 'an obstinate silence' (Malone).

91. *opinion* v. G.

98–9. *If they...brothers fools* They would utter such stupidities that those who heard them would inevitably call them fools and so risk damnation. A reference to Matth. v. 22, the word 'brothers' being a direct echo of the text.

100. *time.* So Q.

101–102. *fish not...opinion* Cf. *Troil.* 4. 4. 105–106

> Whiles others fish with craft for great opinion,
> I with great truth catch mere simplicity.

105. *dinner-time.* So Q.

110. *Fare you well* a dissyllable in rapid speech.
for this gear v. G. 'gear.'

112. *tongue* (Q. 1619) Q. 'togue'
S.D. Q. 'Exeunt.' F. 'Exit.' It is noteworthy that these 112 lines, the quantity which Shakespeare normally took to cover two sides of a foolscap leaf, conclude with an 'exeunt,' which often denotes 'exeunt omnes,' and are followed by a patch of prose, the only prose in the whole scene. In other words it looks as if there had been adaptation here. Cf. p. 112.

113. *Is that* (Rowe) Q. 'It is that'

119—21. *what lady...tell me of* Cf. note 1. 1. 1.

126—27. *Nor do...noble rate* i.e. nor am I now complaining at having to cut down my lordly style of living. Cf. G. 'rate.'

128. *fairly* i.e. honourably.

129. *time* i.e. time of life, youth.

136—37. *stand...Within the eye of honour* i.e. 'lies within the scope of honour's vision' (Aldis Wright). *still*=ever, always (not 'yet' as some edd. interpret).

145. *pure innocence* i.e. pure foolishness. Thus Bassanio describes, in advance, his projected visit to Belmont! He is not an attractive character; but his embarrassment in this scene is obvious, and may have been caused in part by consciousness of the cause of Antonio's melancholy. Cf. note 1. 1. 1.

151. *back* Q. 'bake'

162. *and fairer than that word* i.e. and what is better still.

171. *strand* Q. 'strond'—a Shakespearian spelling.

185. *of my trust or for my sake* i.e. on my credit or for friendship sake.
S.D. Q. 'Exeunt.'

1. 2.

S.D. Q. 'Enter Portia with her wayting woman Nerriffa.'

9. *sentences* v. G.

15. *than be* (F.) Q. 'than to be'

21–2. *whom...whom* (F.) Q. 'who...who'

31. *whom you* (Pope) Q. 'who you'

34 et seq. *I pray thee over-name them* etc. Shakespeare is here quite clearly returning to and developing the conversation between Julia and her maid in *The Two Gentlemen*, 1. 2. 4–15.

37–9. *Neapolitan...talk of his horse* The Neapolitans were recognised in Shakespeare's day as 'the schoolmasters of all Europe in the art of horsemanship' and the practice of the manage was introduced into England by Henry VIII direct from Naples (Sh.Eng. ii. 409, 412).

43. *Then* (Q. 1619) Q. 'Than' This form (which is also found at 2. 2. 188; 3. 2. 48; 3. 5. 46; 4. 1. 241) is unusual and worthy of note.

44. *frown, as* Q. 'frowne (as'—the other bracket occurs after 'youth' l. 48.

45. *choose!* v. G.

47. *the weeping philosopher* The nickname of Heraclitus of Ephesus.

52. *Le Bon* (Capell) Q. 'Le Boune' Cf. *L.L.L.* note 5. 1. 27–9.

57. *throstle* Q. 'Traffel'

59. *shadow*. So Q.

69–71. *I think he bought...every where* Marshall quotes Greene, *Farewell to Follie* (1591): 'I haue seene an English gentleman so defused in his sutes, his doublet being for the weare of Castile, his hose for Venice, his hat for France, his cloake for Germanie.'

72. *Scottish* The F. reads 'other' in deference to the susceptibilities of James I, who saw the play on Feb. 10, 1605, and liked it so well that it was acted again before him two days later. Jonson and Chapman got into serious trouble later on in the same year apparently for a passage reflecting on the Scots in *Eastward Ho!* v. E. K. Chambers, *Eliz. Stage*, iii. pp. 254–55.

77–8. *the Frenchman...sealed under for another* 'Alluding to the constant assistance, or rather constant promises of assistance, that the French gave the Scots in their quarrels with the English' (Warburton). The 'for another' means 'for another box on the ear: the principal was said to "seal to" a bond; his surety to "seal under"' (Aldis Wright).

99. *than* (F. 'then') Q. 'the' for 'thẽ'

116. S.D. Q. 'Enter a Seruingman.'

118. *The four strangers* 'It may be presumed that the number originally [i.e. in the pre-Shakespearian play] was only four, and that the two added on a revisal were the English and Scottish lords, the better to please an English audience' (Hunter, *New Illustrations*, i. p. 322). Cf. p. 113.

125. *the complexion of a devil* i.e. black. Cf. *Oth.* 5. 2. 131 'And you the blacker devil.' The modern Devil is red; in Shakespeare's day he was black.

127–28. The rhyme doggerel, which is printed as prose by Q., probably dates back to the pre-Shakespearian play.

128. S.D. Q. 'Exeunt.'

I. 3.

S.D. Q. 'Enter Baſſanio with Shylocke the Iew.' Shylock's speeches in this scene at ll. 28, 31, 38 are headed 'Iew,' the rest are headed with abbreviations of his name. Cf. pp. 94–5.

1–12. It is noteworthy that the longer speeches in this rapid dialogue are broken up into short lengths in the Quarto. Thus ll. 4–5 are divided: 'For the which ...told you,/Anthonio...bound.'

1. *well*. Some edd. read 'well?' Shylock is assenting, not questioning. Possibly he is intended to be writing in his 'tables' as he speaks; if so the 'well' marks the period at the end of each note he makes.

19. *Rialto* (F2) Q. 'Ryalta' But Q. prints 'Ryalto' at ll. 36, 104. Completed in 1591, and therefore a novelty; cf. F. L. Lucas, *Works of Webster*, i. p. 233.

21. *hath squandered* Theobald reads 'hath, squandered' There is no comma in Q.

23. *land-thieves and water-thieves* (Singer) Q. 'water theeues, and land theeues' Singer's order seems certain, seeing that 'I mean pirates' follows. Transposition is one of the commonest of misprints, and would be especially easy after 'land-rats and water-rats.'

31–5. *Yes, to smell pork...pray with you* We take this as an aside, while Shylock is apparently 'bethinking' himself (cf. l. 29). It would be unlike the Jew to reveal his hate openly at this stage, while 'What news on the Rialto' makes an obvious re-entry into conversation. Shylock, of course, accepts an invitation to supper later on.

32. *Nazarite* This is given for 'Nazarene' in Matth. ii. 23 in most versions of the Bible before the A.V. of 1611.

36. S.D. Q. 'Enter Anthonio.'

37. After 36 lines of prose, we begin verse—with a broken line. We suspect the change to be connected with the second revision.

38. *fawning publican* The Pharisee unwittingly compares Antonio, who enters sadly and with downcast eyes, with the Publican of the parable.

40. *low simplicity* i.e. foolish humility.

43. *upon the hip* v. G. 'hip' and Sh.Hand, p. 166 *n*.

49. *Shylock* Q. 'Shyloch'

63. *And for three months* A short line, but no metrical break.

66. *Methoughts* Q. 'Me thoughts'.

72–4. *interest* 'If, when Shakespeare produced *The Merchant of Venice*, in 1594, interest was still a word of such ill omen that the popular Antonio could find no stronger term with which to stigmatize the "bargains and the well-won thrift" of Shylock, this was not because the practice of taking it was uncommon, but because in one form or other it was becoming universal. In the social problems of that period the question of interest occupied the same central position as the question of wages occupies in the social problems of to-day' (Prof. Unwin, Sh. Eng. i. 332). Q. gives the successive spellings 'interrest,' 'interest,' 'intrest.' Cf. the five different spellings of 'sheriff' in the 'Shakespearian' Addition to *Sir Thomas More*, ll. 41–5.

74–87. *mark what Jacob did* etc. Cf. Gen. xxx. 31–43. Shylock's argument is that as Jacob thrived, and received God's blessing for thriving, in the breeding of sheep, so it was lawful to make money breed.

75. *compromised* Q. 'compremyzed'—a Shakespearian spelling, cf. *M.W.W.* note 1. 1. 30.

80. *woolly* Q. 'wolly'

81. *pilled* Q. 'pyled' The collateral forms 'pill' and 'peel' were synonymous in all senses down to the 17th cent. v. N.E.D. Cf. *Meas.* G. 'pile.'

88. *served for*— Q. 'ſerued for.'

99. *goodly* Rowe reads 'godly' The words 'good' and 'god' are confused elsewhere in the Qq. (cf. *M.N.D.* 2. 2. 51 note), while the compositor might also be influenced by 'goodly' in l. 98.

109, 123, 128. *spit* (F2) Q. 'spet', this being a common 16th cent. form for the verb in both present and past tenses. Cf. 2. 7. 45.

113. *say so!* Q. 'ſay ſo;'

116. *suit.* So Q.

128. *thee too.* Q. 'thee to.'

131. *A breed for barren metal* Antonio refers to one of the stock arguments of the age (which goes back to Aristotle) concerning usury, viz. 'that it is against Nature for money to beget money' (Bacon, *Of Usurie*).

139. short line, probably deliberate.

142. *your single bond* v. G. 'single bond.'

145. *the forfeit* That a pound of man's flesh should

be nominated as a forfeit, 'in a merry sport,' would seem
far less strange in Shakespeare's day than in ours. One
is reminded of peppercorn rents which still survive
from those times, or of the commodities 'of brown
paper and old ginger' by which the usurers circum-
vented the law in restriction of interest. Cf. *Meas.* G.
'commodity.'

158. *dealing teaches* (F2) Q. 'dealings teaches'
The harshness of 'dealings teaches' persuades us that
this 'northern plural,' as it is called, belonged to the
compositor not to Shakespeare.

174. *I will* (Theobald) Q. 'Ile' S.D. Q. 'Exit.'

174-75. Q. divides 'Hie thee…will turne/Chriſtian
…kinde' Possibly the speech was written in one line
in the MS in order to crowd the end of the scene into
the foot of a page. Cf. *L.L.L.* p. 123.

175. *The Hebrew* (Q.) Most edd. follow F. and
read 'This Hebrew'

178. S.D. Q. 'Exeunt.'

2. 1.

S.D. Q. 'Enter Morochus a tawnie Moore all in
white, and three or foure followers accordingly, with
Portia, Nerriſſa, and their traine.' This, the most
elaborate S.D. in the Q., is obviously theatrical in
origin. But once again it differs from the dialogue, in
the spelling of 'Morocco.' Cf. p. 99. F. adds 'Flo.
Cornets.'

2. *The shadowed livery* an expression from heraldry;
v. G. 'shadowed' and 'livery.' Blake without a thought
of heraldry utters the same idea in his *Little Black Boy*:

> And these black bodies and this sunburnt face
> Is but a cloud, and like a shady grove.

3. *bred.* So Q.   7. *mine.* So Q.

6. *make incision for your love* The parallel with
L.L.L. 4. 3. 92-5 suggests that the fever of love may
have been sometimes treated by the surgeon.

7. *reddest* Red blood is a traditional sign of courage (Johnson). Cf. ll. 8–9.

9. *valiant. By my love, I swear* Q. 'valiant, (by my loue I ſweare)'

11. *it too* Q. 'it to'

27. *o'erstare* Most edd. follow Q. 1619 and read 'out-stare'

31. *thee, lady* Q. 'the lady'

35. *page* (Theobald and edd.) Q. 'rage'. J.D.W. 1926 'wag'. C.J.S. 'rogue'. J.D.W. and C.J.S. (*New Readings*, i, 136–137) follow the ductus litterarum but the sense of the context supports 'page' which emphasizes the contrast in size between giant and boy, so does 'wag'=boy; but 'page' is best because it also suggests the relation between boy and Sir Hercules; 'rogue' does neither. In the compositor's lower case the 'p' is just above the 'r'. [1962].

44. *forward to the temple* i.e. to take the oath.

46. S.D. Q. 'Exeunt.' F. reads 'Cornets.' at the end of l. 45.

2. 2.

This scene is so peculiar from the bibliographical point of view that a textual analysis of it must be attempted, thus: (i) ll. 1–29, the opening speech of Lancelot, headed 'Clowne' in Q.; (ii) ll. 30–142, prose throughout including Bassanio's speeches, while all Lancelot's speeches are prefixed with his own name. The matter in these first two sections, being prose, would just about cover two sides of a foolscap sheet of script; (iii) ll. 143–203, Bassanio speaks verse throughout, Lancelot's speeches are headed 'Clowne,' and at l. 167 the mysterious Leonardo makes his unexpected appearance (cf. p. 110). This third section, which runs to 60 lines, may be taken we think to represent a page of material partly pre-Shakespearian and partly revised, copied out in 1594. It is to be noted that prose which was once verse links §§ (ii) and (iii) together. Thus

ll. 140–41 together make up a line of verse, and l. 142,
if the word 'sir' be omitted, is also verse. Further Dyce
pronounced Gratiano's speech at l. 175 'beyond doubt,
originally verse.' Whether the alternation of 'Clowne'
and 'Launcelet' speech-headings is connected with revision or was due to the typographical exigencies of
Roberts' printing-office (cf. pp. 94–5) we must leave
an open question.

S.D. Q. 'Enter the Clowne alone.'

3–8. *Gobbo, Lancelot Gobbo* etc. Q. 'Iobbe,
Launcelet Iobbe' etc. Both Prof. A. W. Pollard and
Prof. Moore Smith have independently suggested
privately that Q. gives us here a phonetic spelling of
'Giobbe,' the Italian equivalent to 'Job'; and there
can be little doubt that they are right. The fact that Q.
prints 'Gobbo' in the S.D. at l. 29 and in the subsequent speech-headings indicates, we think, a different
hand from that originally responsible for the dialogue.
Cf. p. 99.

8–9. *scorn running with thy heels* A quibble, 'to
scorn with the heels' meaning apparently 'to spurn,' v.
Ado, G. 'scorn.'

10. *Fia!* i.e. via (v. G.). We retain the Q. form
because Shakespeare always gives 'via' elsewhere and
there is probably a word-play upon 'fi-end' following.

11. *for the heavens* v. G. 'heavens.'

12–13. *hanging about the neck of my heart* i.e. like
the timid wife or mistress—a variant of Hamlet's
'conscience doth make cowards of us all.'

22. *God bless the mark!* v. G. 'mark.'

25. *devil incarnation* Cf. Mistress Quickly's blunder,
Hen. V, 2. 3. 35.

29. S.D. Q. 'Enter old Gobbo with a basket.' His
speeches are all headed 'Gobbo' or some contraction
of the name. v. p. 99.

30. *young-man* The hyphen and the punctuation,
of course, come from Q.

33. *high gravel-blind* A correspondent (Mr S. E. Preston) suggests 'nigh' for 'high' and the emendation has some attractions though it would have more if it could be shown that the compositor's case was foul in respect of the *n* and *h* boxes. 'Gravel-blind' as Capell remarks, is Lancelot's half-way stage between 'sand-blind' and 'stone-blind.'

34. *confusions* Lancelot's attempt to 'confuse' old Gobbo immediately after shows that he uses this word deliberately.

41. *Be God's sonties* All mod. edd. follow F4 and read 'By' for the vulgar 'Be' For 'sonties' v. G.

52. *Your worship's friend and Lancelot, sir* A common form when repudiating an unmerited title. Cf. *L.L.L.* 5. 2. 568 'Your servant, and Costard,' where Costard is deprecating the title of 'Pompey the Great.'

53. *ergo* We take this to be intended for a verb in the imperative: 'draw the logical conclusion, I pray you,' says Lancelot.

54. *talk you of young Master Lancelot.* Many edd. printed this as a question. It seems to us better to follow the Q. pointing and take it as imperative.

57. *father* a natural form of address to any old man.

68. *God* Q. prints as 'GOD' v. p. 173.

76. *murder* Q. 'muder'

90–91. *Lord worshipped...he be!* It is not clear whether this is intended for a mere expletive or whether the words 'might he be' refer to Lancelot.

92. *fill-horse* (Pope) Q. 'philhorſe' v. G.

94. *backward.* So Q.

95. *last* (Q. 1619) Q. 'loſt'

103. *service....* The Q. period denotes stage-business; probably the traditional action by which Lancelot seizes his father's hand and brings it into contact with the fingers of his own left hand which are extended rib-like over his chest.

109. *S.D.* Q. 'Enter Baffanio with a follower or two.' For 'Leonardo' v. l. 167 below.

111–12. *supper...five of the clock* Elizabethans usually ate supper about 5.30 p.m. v. Sh.Eng. ii. 134.

113–14. *desire Gratiano...lodging* This looks like a 'loose end' seeing that Gratiano enters at l. 171 of the present scene (v. note).

114. *S.D.* Q. gives none. Q. 1619 reads 'Exit one of his men.'

119. *Here's my son* Q. heads this 'Gobbe'

123. *infection* i.e. affection.

131. *the Jew having done me wrong* This suggests that Lancelot may have had some more definite cause of complaint than appears in the present text.

144. *Shylock...this day* There is nothing in 1. 3. about this; cf. note l. 131 above.

148. *The old proverb* i.e. 'God's grace is gear enough.'

155. *Father, in* This shows that the scene is supposed to be just outside Shylock's house.

157–58. *if any man in Italy...good fortune* This has puzzled critics. We paraphrase: 'If any man in Italy hath a fairer palm than mine—a palm which not only promises but offers to swear upon a book that I shall have good fortune—' Lancelot would have added 'I'll be hanged' or some such phrase but that his enthusiasm at the vision of his palm carried him away. The idea of a palm offering 'to swear upon a book' is explained by Johnson thus: 'The act of expanding his hand puts him in mind of the action in which the palm is shown by raising it to lay it on the book, in judicial attestations.' For 'table' v. G.

160. *eleven* Q. 'a leuen'—a Shakespearian spelling. v. Sh.Hand, p. 126.

162–63. *in peril...feather-bed* This sounds an excellent jest, but no one has yet been able to explain it.

166. *in the twinkling* Q. 1619 adds (unnecessarily) 'of an eye', and all edd. follow.

S.D. Q. 'Exit Clowne.'

167. *Leonardo* This 'Leonardo' crops up very un-expectedly in the Q. text. No entry is provided for him; he has a line and a half to say in reply to Bassanio and Gratiano; and then goes out, never to appear again. We take him to be a relic of the old text, v. p. 110.

171. S.D. Q. 'Exit Leonardo'—though he does not actually go off until two lines later. 'Enter Gratiano.'

172. *Where's* So Q. Many mod. edd. read 'Where is'

174. *have a suit* (Q. 1619) Q. 'haue fute'

177. *you* Q. 'yon'

178. *too wild, too rude* Q. 'to wild, to rude'

180. *faults;* Q. 'faults'

181. *known,* Q. 'knowne;'

188. *then* Q. 'than' Cf. note 1. 2. 43.

195, 201. broken lines; possibly due to some abridgment at the end of the scene.

203. S.D. Q. 'Exeunt.'

2. 3.

We doubt whether anything in this scene, except the speech of Lancelot's, is Shakespeare's; cf. p. 110.

S.D. Q. 'Enter Ieffica and the Clowne.'

5. *soon at* v. G.

9, 15. short lines, which suggest that Lancelot's speech was originally verse; cf. p. 110.

10. *exhibit* probably a blunder for 'inhibit' (Aldis Wright).

14. Q. gives no 'exit'; Q. 1619 and F. supply it.

20. *strife* i.e. between her duty as a daughter and her love for Lorenzo.

21. S.D. Q. 'Exit.'

2. 4.

S.D. Q. 'Enter Gratiano, Lorenfo, Salaryno, and

Salanio.' The speech-headings give us 'Salari.,' 'Sal.'
and 'Solanio,' 'Sol.' Cf. pp. 100–104.

1. *slink away in supper-time* This was evidently the
practice in Shakespeare's day at these impromptu
maskings. Exactly the same thing happens in *Much Ado*
(2. 1.), where Don Pedro and his party of men, after
taking supper with Leonato and his household, go out,
mask themselves, and return for a dance (cf. *Ado*, note
2. 1. 76). The masquers generally disguised themselves
as foreigners. In *L.L.L.* (5. 2.) they appear as Russians,
in *Hen. VIII* as shepherds who can 'speak no English'
(1. 4. 65). Their advent was frequently announced by
a 'herald' (cf. *Rom.* 1. 4. 3–8; *L.L.L.* 5. 2. 97–108;
157 S.D.; *Hen. VIII*, 1. 4. 63 S.D., 65–72), and they
were accompanied by attendants bearing torches (cf.
Rom. 1. 4. 11–12, 35–39). As they entered they were
preceded by a drum and fife (cf. below 2. 5. 29–30,
Rom. 1. 4. 114; *Ado*, note 2. 1. 76). See also E. K.
Chambers, *Elizabethan Stage*, ch. v.

3. *All in an hour* a broken line, printed with l. 2
in Q. It suggests that a passage about the masque has
been 'cut'; we do not actually learn that a masque is
afoot until l. 22.

5. *spoke as yet of* (Rowe) Q. 'ſpoke vs yet of'
If the 'of' were away, 'spoke us' might mean 'be-
spoken'; as it is, Rowe's emendation is certainly
correct. An *a*:*u* misprint, v. T.I. p. xli and Sh.Hand,
p. 118.

torch-bearers Cf. note l. 1 above.

8. *o'clock* (Q. 1619 'a clocke') Q. 'of clocke'
Probably the 'of' is due to compositor's normalising.

9. S.D. Q. 'Enter Launcelet.' F. adds 'with a
Letter.' The clown's speeches in this scene are headed
'Launcelet' or 'Launce' by Q.

11. *break up this* Cf. G. 'break up,' *L.L.L.* 4. 1. 56,
and *Wint.* 3. 2. 130.

13. *paper it writ on* Hanmer read 'paper that it

writ on' A contracted 'that' (=y^t) might easily be overlooked with 'it' (=yt) following.

14. *Love-news* Q. 'Loue, newes'

17–18. *to bid...the Christian* This invitation, only two hours before the supper actually takes place, has nothing to do with the invitation to dinner at 1. 3. 30, as some commentators have assumed. Its purpose, we suppose, was to get Shylock out of the way so as to facilitate Jessica's escape; if so, it forms part of the masquing plot, the details of which have been cut away in revision. Cf. pp. 110–11.

20. S.D. Q. 'Exit Clowne.' after l. 23.

21. *Go, gentlemen,* Q. prints this broken line with l. 22. Once again we have a 'cut' relating to the masque.

25–6. Q. prints 'Meete me...lodging/Some houre hence.' This arrangement, and the broken line that follows, point once more to adaptation.

27. broken line. S.D. Q. 'Exit.'

35. *dare* i.e. will dare. Some interpret the passage as a wish, viz. 'May misfortune never dare'; but surely a wish from Lorenzo in these terms would admit of no possible exceptions. *her foot* i.e. her path.

39. S.D. Q. 'Exit.'

2. 5.

S.D. Q. 'Enter Iewe and his man that was the Clowne.' Cf. p. 105. Q. 1619 deletes 'his man... Clowne' and substitutes 'Lancelet.' Q. heads Shylock's first speech 'Iewe' and those that follow 'Shy.'; Lancelot's speeches are headed 'Clowne.'

3. *gormandise* For Lancelot's side of the story cf. 2. 2. 102–104.

8–9. *Your worship...bidding* Q. prints this in two short lines.

9. S.D. Q. 'Enter Ieffica.'

11. *bid forth to supper* Cf. note 2. 4. 17–18.

18. *dream of money-bags* Aldis Wright quotes 'Some say that to dreame of money, and all kinde of coyne is ill' (Artemidorus, *The Judgement or Exposition of Dreams,* ed. 1616).

22. *And they have* Some edd. read 'An they have' In the old texts 'an' is of course always printed 'and'

23–7. *it was not for nothing* etc. Lancelot's prognostications mock Shylock's dream about the money-bags.

29–30. *the drum...fife* Cf. note 2. 4. 1.

33. *varnished faces* This seems to have puzzled critics, but it is clearly a reference to the visors of the masquers. These visors were often grotesque (cf. *Ado,* 2. 1. 85–6 note).

39–40. *I will go before* etc. Lancelot speaks a line and a half of verse. We follow Q. arrangement: all mod. edd. print as prose. We regard this as an important clue as to revision; cf. pp. 110–11.

42. *Jewess' eye* Q. 'Iewes eye' v. G. 'Jew's eye.' Q. gives no 'exit.'

53. *Fast bind, fast find* Q. prints this with l. 52.

54, 56. S.D. Q. 'Exit.'

2. 6.

S.D. Q. 'Enter the maskers, Gratiano and Salerino.' For 'Salerino' Q. 1619 reads 'Salarino' and F. 'Salino.'

1. *pent-house* The actor who played Gratiano on Shakespeare's stage spoke the literal truth here, since the 'heavens' which protected the back of the stage from the elements was surmounted by a thatched pent-house. Cf. E. K. Chambers, *Eliz. Stage,* ii. 544. Shakespeare uses 'pent-house' in a similar connexion in *Ado,* 3. 3. 101.

5. *Venus' pigeons* which, of course, draw the goddess' chariot in her flight 'to seal love's bonds.'

7. *obligèd faith* v. G.

10—11. *untread...tedious measures* referring to the complicated motions of the horse in the manage: 'measures'=lit. paces in a dance.

13. *enjoyed.* Q. 'enioyd.'   14. *younger* v. G.

16. *the strumpet wind* The reference, of course, is to the harlots with whom the 'younger,' or Prodigal, wasted his substance.

19. S.D. Q. 'Enter Lorenzo.'

24. short line—possibly a 'cut' here.

25. S.D. Q. 'Ieſſica aboue.' i.e. on the upper-stage. Cf. p. 105.

28. another short line, but probably deliberate.

42. *light.* So Q.

46. *But come at once* yet another broken line, this time in the middle of a speech and undoubtedly, we think, caused by a 'cut.'

50. S.D. Q. gives no 'exit.'

51. *by my hood* 'Gratiano is in a masqued habit, to which it is probable that formerly, as at present, a large cape or hood was affixed' (Malone). The expression, though not found elsewhere in Shakespeare, was not uncommon. Its origin is unknown. If Malone be correct, Gratiano is quibbling.

gentle a quibble of course upon 'Gentile' (cf. note 4. 1. 34): the two words were not distinguished in spelling at this date.

57. S.D. Q. 'Enter Ieſſica.'

58—9. *What, art thou come?* etc. This dismissal-couplet looks like the original end to the scene. Cf. p. 111.

59. S.D. Q. 'Exit.'/'Enter Anthonio.'

68. S.D. Q. 'Exeunt.'

2. 7.

S.D. Q. 'Enter Portia with Morrocho and both theyr traines.'

3. broken line—possibly a 'cut' here.

18. *threatens. Men* (Rowe) Q. 'threatens men'

23, 31, 38, 40, 43, 48. Q. prints a full-stop at the end of each of these lines.

34. *deserve* (Q.) Capell reads 'deserve her' With 'here' at the end of the next line, a compositor might easily have overlooked 'her'

40. *shrine* v. G. *mortal-breathing* v. G.

41. *Hyrcanian* Q. 'Hircanian'

44. *The watery kingdom* Morocco means, of course, the ocean.

45. *Spits* (F2) Q. 'Spets'. Cf. note 1. 3. 109. For 'spits in the face of heaven' cf. *Temp.* 1. 2. 4. 'The sea, mounting to th' welkin's cheek.'

46. *To stop the foreign spirits* There is a quibble here, inasmuch as according to the superstition of the age 'spirits' were unable to travel easily across water (cf. Sh.Eng. i. 543).

49. *her? 'Twere* Q. 'her twere'

51. *rib her cerecloth* Corpses were commonly wrapped in lead for burial at this period. The passage subtly prepares us for the 'carrion Death' and 'Gilded tombs do worms infold.'

53. *ten times undervalued* Morocco is expressing the exact legal value of silver in terms of gold at the end of the 16th century.

56. *an angel* v. G.

57. *Stampèd* (Rowe) Q. 'ftampt'
insculped upon v. G.

57–9. *insculped upon...Lies all within* The emphatic words here are 'upon' (=outside) and 'within'

62–4. Q. divides 'O hell! what...death/within... fcroule,/Ile...writing'—which suggests marginal revision, and possibly abridgment.

62. *here* Q. 'heare'

63. *A carrion Death* v. G. 'carrion.'

65–73. The scroll which Q. prints in italics. We take this, together with Arragon's and Bassanio's scrolls,

as belonging to the pre-Shakespearian play; cf. p. 113.
The lines are tiresome and obscure.

68. *my outside* The 'outside' of the 'carrion Death'
is, of course, the golden casket. But more than that is
intended; the 'outside' includes all the 'outward shows'
of life upon which Bassanio comments in 3. 2. 73–101.

69. *Gilded tombs* etc. The reference is to Matth.
xxiii. 27 'like unto whited (marg. 'or painted') tombes,
which appeare beautiful outward, but are within full
of dead men's bones and of all filthines' (Genevan
version). 'Gilded' and 'painted' come very near
together.

tombs (Johnson) Q. 'timber' For the confusion
between final *s* and *r* cf. *L.L.L.* 3. 1. 179 Iunios (for
'Iunior') and Sh.Hand, plate vi.

73. *Fare you well...cold* This is, of course, the 'in-
scrolled' answer. For 'cold' v. G.

74. Q. gives this line a fresh prefix '*Mor.*' Cf.
pp. 96–9, and notes 2. 9. 73; 3. 2. 62 S.D., 131–38.

75. *farewell heat, and welcome frost* an 'inversion of
the common old proverb, "Farewell frost," which was
used on the absence or departure of anything that was
unwelcome or displeasing' (Halliwell).

77. *part* i.e. depart. S.D. Q. 'Exit.'

79. S.D. Q. 'Exeunt.'

2. 8.

S.D. Q. 'Enter Salarino and Solanio.' Q. 1619
reads 'Salanio' for 'Solanio.' F. adds 'Flo. Cornets';
probably this S.D. was written in the margin of the Q.
by the book-holder in such a way that the F. compositor was left in doubt whether it belonged to 2. 8.
or to the end of 2. 7. The 'cornets,' of course, sounded
for Morocco's exit. The Q. prefixes for 'Salarino' and
'Solanio' are 'Sal.' and 'Sol.' throughout.

8. *gondola* Q. 'Gondylo'—possibly Shakespeare's
spelling.

9. *Jessica.* So Q.

15–22. We follow mod. edd. in supplying notes of exclamation to this agitated speech.

39. *Slubber* (Q. 1619 and F.) Q. 'flumber' Perhaps the compositor or the transcriber took 'sluber' for 'slŭber' For 'slubber' v. G.

42. *mind of love* v. G.

46–50. *his eye being big with tears* etc. What is the meaning of this 'affection wondrous sensible,' if it be not caused by the prospect of Bassanio's marriage? Solanio's comment 'I think he only loves the world for him' and the linking up of Antonio's 'embracéd heaviness' with the parting from Bassanio seem to leave no other alternative. Cf. note 1. 1. 1.

52. *embracéd heaviness* Cf. 'rash-embraced despair' 3. 2. 109.

53. S.D. Q. 'Exeunt.'

2. 9.

S.D. Q. 'Enter Neriſſa and a Seruiture.' Theatrical attendants in the Elizabethan playhouse were called 'servitors,' and it was current gossip in the 17th century that Shakespeare himself had joined the stage as a 'serviture' (cf. E. K. Chambers, *Eliz. Stage*, ii. 541, *n*. 3). Chambers (iii. 81) is uncertain 'whether the "servitours" of a theatre ever came upon the stage, undisguised, to draw the curtains.' The Q. text of *M.V.*, with its playhouse stage-directions, suggests that they did; but perhaps, like the attendants in a modern circus, they wore a uniform which would blend naturally with those of the actors in any play.

2. *ta'en his oath* i.e. at the temple; cf. 2. 1. 44.

3. S.D. Q. 'Enter Arrogon, his trayne, and Portia.' F. adds 'Flor. Cornets.'

14. *Lastly* This extra-metrical word, printed along with l. 15 by Q., almost certainly denotes abridgment.

N.B. the clumsy repetition of 'If I do fail' (l. 15) so shortly after 'if I fail' (l. 11).

21. *hath*. So Q.

26. *the fool multitude, that choose by show* It is note-worthy, in view of Shakespeare's reputed dislike of the common people, that he places these contemptuous words in the mouth of a pompous ass. On the other hand, the sentiment is closely paralleled by that in the lines

And what the people but a herd confused,
A miscellaneous rabble, who extol
Things vulgar, and, well weighed, scarce worth the praise,

which Milton attributes to Christ in *Par. Reg.* iii. 49–51. On the whole question of Shakespeare's political opinions, see the important article by Prof. R. W. Chambers, ch. 5, Sh.Hand.

30. *casualty*. So Q.

46. *gleaned* v. G.

48. *Picked* v. G. *chaff* (Q. 1619) Q. 'chaft'

ruin v. G. *times* with a quibble on 'temse,' a fine sieve for bolting meal.

49. *varnished* Critics have commented upon the confusion of metaphors involved in the use of this word. We suspect that Shakespeare is continuing the quibble on 'times,' but can suggest no meaning for 'varnished' suitable to grain, or meal.

51. *I will assume desert* To take this in the modern sense of the words is to miss the whole point. Arragon seizes upon the casket as if it were the insignia of his office, saying, 'I will take to me that which I deserve.' v. G. 'assume.'

53. *Too long a pause* etc. We follow Capell in making this an 'aside.'

62. Q. 1619 adds S.D. 'Hee reads.'

63–72. The scroll. Q. prints in italics. Cf. pp. 96–9.

64. *judgement* Q. 'iudement'

73. *Still more fool* etc. Q. heads this '*Arrag.*' v. pp. 96–9.

78. *roth* (Dyce) Q. 'wroath' It seems now generally agreed that 'ruth' is intended, with a spelling to make an eye-rhyme to 'oath.' v. G. 'roth.' Possibly the *w* was introduced by the players who mistook the word for a form of 'wrath.' Q. gives no 'exit.'

84. *Come...Nerissa.* This line of prose which suddenly crops up in the middle of a verse-scene points to à 'cut.'

S.D. Q. 'Enter Meſſenger.'

85. *my lady...my lord* Cf. *L.L.L.* 5. 2. 239; 1 *Hen IV*, 2. 4. 314; *Ric. II*, 5. 5. 67. There was evidently something about this kind of retort which tickled the Elizabethans.

92. *love.* So Q.

101. *Bassanio—Lord Love* Q. 'Baſſanio Lord, loue' Rowe read 'Bassanio, lord Love' The messenger has not named the 'lord' of the 'young Venetian,' but it is obvious that both Portia and Nerissa think at once of Bassanio. The maid alone expresses these thoughts in this prayer to 'Lord Love.'

S.D. Q. 'Exeunt.' Q. 1619 'Exit.'

3. 1.

S.D. Q. 'Solanio and Salarino.' Q. 1619 and F. add 'Enter'; Q. 1619 reads 'Salanio' for 'Solanio.' The Q. prefixes in the scene for these two characters are 'Solanio,' 'Solan.,' 'Sola.' and 'Salari.' (7 times), 'Saleri.' (once) respectively.

15. *Come, the full stop* Salerio refers here not only to the period but to the 'stop' in the manage: Solanio is a colt whose 'career' must be checked (cf. Sh.Eng. ii. 414).

20. *my prayer* i.e. the 'amen' he has just uttered.

21. S.D. Q. 'Enter Shylocke' after l. 22.

22–35. How easily, with a little alteration, this passage would go into verse, thus:

Sol. How now, Shylock! what news among the merchants?
Shy. You knew, none so well, none so well as you,
    Of my daughter's flight.
Sal.   I, for my part, knew
    The tailor made the wings she flew withal.
Sol. And Shylock for his part knew the bird was fledge,
    And then 'tis the complexion of them all
    To leave the dam.
Shy.   She is damnéd for it!
Sal. That's certain, if the devil may be her judge.
Shy. My own flesh and blood to rebel!
Sol.   Out upon it!
    Old carrion, rebels it at these years?
Shy. I say, my daughter is my flesh and blood.

This may not be exactly how Shakespeare's manuscript once read, but we are persuaded it is something like it.

28. *fledge* (Capell) Q. 'flidge' v. G. Most edd. follow Q. 1619 and read 'fledged'

46. *curtsy* Q. 'curfie' A quibble. v. G. Most edd. read 'courtesy' The Q. text is far more forcible.

64. *humility* v. G.

67. S.D. Q. 'Enter a man from Anthonio.' This S.D. reminds one of the locality S.D.s of *Errors* (p. 72). There is no speech-heading to the 'man's' lines, and the scribe presumably drew upon the words 'my master Antonio' for the clue to the entry. Cf. next note.

68. *Gentlemen* etc. Q. gives no prefix. We suggest that the transcript lacked one, because the lines would belong to a small-part actor, who played several parts, his lines being strung together on a strip and perhaps headed with his own name.

The message, to which in Q. 'Saleri.' replies, makes the identification of 'Saleri' with 'Salerio' practically certain. Cf. pp. 100–104.

70. S.D. Q. 'Enter Tuball.'

72. S.D. Q. 'Exeunt Gentlemen.'/'Enter Tuball.'

Q. 1619 and F. omit 'Enter Tuball.' The duplication
of stage-directions by different scribes is common in
prompt-books of the period (cf. *Errors*, p. 73). One of
the two entries for Tubal may, for instance, have been
supplied by the scribe who added the S.D.s for *The
Merchant* transcript (v. pp. 103–104), and the other by
the book-holder at some performance at which the
transcript was used as prompt-copy.

100. *Heard in Genoa?* (Neilson and Hill, Alexander,
C.J.S.) Q. 'heere in Genowa?' Rowe and most edd.
'Where in Genoa?'—which is pointless. C.J.S. (*New
Readings*, i, 139–140) explains Q. 'heere' as misreading
of 'herd' (a spel. of 'heard') and Alexander (*Sh. Survey*
5, p. 5) does likewise. Shylock repeats Tubal's 'heard
in Genoa' (l. 91) in the hope of receiving more good
news. [1962].

118. *officer* v. G.

121. *meet me at our synagogue* This is no token of
hypocrisy as some have imagined. Shylock goes thither
(as the suitors at Belmont go to the 'temple') to take
his oath.

122. S.D. Q. 'Exeunt.'

3. 2.

S.D. Q. 'Enter Baffanio, Portia, Gratiano, and all
their traynes.'

1. *I pray you tarry, pause a day or two* Portia's
opening speech, parts of which have puzzled critics, is
quite clear if the situation at the beginning of the scene
be borne in mind. It is obvious from ll. 24–9 that
Bassanio has made ardent protestation of his love.
Portia's duty is to remain neutral; but she lets him see
she loves him without saying so. Naturally her speech
is more guarded, and therefore more embarrassed (or is

she merely playful?), at the beginning than towards the
end. Note how the 'day or two' lengthens out into 'some
month or two' (l. 9)

7 *But lest...understand me well* i.e. she advises him
to learn to know her better before he hazards, but, of
course, the advice is a mere pretext which deceives
neither Bassanio nor herself.

15. *o'er-looked* v. G   19. *Put* (F2) Q puts

20. *Prove it so* i.e. should it prove so. Q. '(proue it
fo)' This is one of those pieces of punctuation which
defy translation into modern symbols. Portia is in
tended to whisper the 'doubtful thought,' and the next
line should, we think, be uttered almost fiercely and
perhaps with a catch in the voice.

21. *not I* i.e. she will not forswear herself.

35. *confess and live* Cf. the prov 'confess and be
hanged.'

42. *Nerissa and the rest...aloof* The command is
natural: Portia does not wish her dependents to watch
her too narrowly during this trying ordeal. But may
there not be a theatrical need for the withdrawal also?
As Mr Richmond Noble has pointed out, the refrain of
the song is taken up by 'all,' i.e. 'all their traynes'
mentioned in the entry at the beginning of the scene
(cf. *Shakespeare's Use of Song*, pp. 47–8). We suppose,
therefore, they go up into the gallery where the musicians
would be seated.

48. *then* Q. 'Than' Cf. note 1. 2. 43.

49–50. *the flourish...new-crownéd monarch* Malone
detected an allusion here to the coronation of Henry IV
of France, 'who was crowned at Chartres in the midst
of his *true* subjects in 1594' (February 27), Rheims
being still in the hands of the rebels. A contemporary
English account of the ceremonies lays great stress upon
the flourish of trumpets, etc., directly the act of coronation was over. Essex was Henry's friend and had fought
for him; his own friend Southampton would, therefore,
be likely to take great interest in the doings at Chartres.

54. *with much more love* Hercules rescued Hesione not for love but in order to win the horses which her father, Laomedon, had promised him.

57. *sacrifice*: Q. 'facrifice,' 58. *wives*, Q. 'wiues:'—transposed pointing.

61. *I live. With much* Q. 'I liue with much'

62. S.D. Q. 'A Song the whilst Baffanio comments on the caskets to himfelfe.' v. pp. 98–9. F. prefixes 'Here Muficke.'

63–72. *Tell me where is Fancy bred* etc. For 'Fancy' v. G. Mr Richmond Noble (cf. note l. 42 above), following Weiss and Verity, justly remarks: 'The tenour of the song is very obvious, the hint is very plain to beware of that which is pleasing to the sight, for it has no substance....Such evidently was the line of thought it suggested to Bassanio, whose sensitiveness of ear was enhanced by his anxiety and by the hazard of fortune he was essaying, for, almost without waiting for the last strains of the song to fade away, he observes very abruptly,

> So may the outward shows be least themselves—
> The world is still deceived with ornament.

A comment clearly enough inspired by the song.' He adds: 'We are to infer one of two things, either that, while she did not actually forswear herself, Portia's feelings were sufficiently human and womanly to make her sail dangerously near the wind, or that Nerissa chose the song cunningly'; and noting that in *Il Pecorone*, the tale on which the play is founded, a lady's-maid gives a hint to the successful lover, he inclines to the latter alternative. Mr Noble's sole caveat, that 'the point is not as obvious as it ought to be in drama,' has been met by Mr A. H. Fox-Strangways, who very pertinently remarks that 'in that age of anagrams and acrostics' the rhymes 'bred,' 'head,' 'nourishéd,' 'engendred' and 'fed' would at once suggest 'lead' to Bassanio, and the

audience, after hearing 'Morocco taunted by all imagin-
able rhymes to 'gold' and Arragon hissed with all the
sibilants that 'silver' suggests would find the point
obvious enough' (*Times Literary Supp.* July 12, 1923).
Furthermore, the sound of the tolling bell and the
reference to Fancy dying 'in the cradle where it lies' both
hint at the lead which ribbed the 'cerecloth' in the
obscure graves of those times. After all this the dramatic
purpose of the song is not likely to be questioned.

66. *Reply, reply.* Q. prints this, without prefix, in
the margin against l. 65. Mr Noble, following a suggestion of Mr W. J. Lawrence, explains the marginal
position as indicative of a refrain, to be borne by 'All';
and we have adopted this arrangement. The song,
Mr Noble holds, should be a solo and not a duet as
many have supposed.

67. *eyes* (F.) Q. 'eye'

68. *Fancy dies...* Q. 'Fancie dies:' The Q. pause
after 'dies', which is the most important word in the
song, is very striking; yet it has been ignored by everyone, even by Mr Noble himself.

71. *I'll begin it* For some reason which we are
unable to explain, Q. prints this in roman and in a line
by itself, the rest of the song being in italics.

73. *So may* etc. For the cause of this abrupt beginning v. note ll. 63–72 above.

77. *evil?* Q. 'euill.'

80. *ornament?* Q. 'ornament:'

81. *vice* (F2) Q. 'voyce' The misprint is difficult
to explain, unless we suppose a phonetic spelling in the
copy, e.g. 'veyce' or 'vayce.' Such spellings were
possible in the 16th cent. (cf. Wyld, *Hist. Mod. Coll.
English*, pp. 223–26; Jespersen, *Mod. Eng. Grammar*,
i. 8. 21), but not we think Shakespearian.

84. *stairs* (F4) Q. 'ftayers' a common 16th cent.
spelling, which recurs in 2 *Hen. IV*, 2. 1. 108.

85. *The beards of Hercules* etc. Cf. Stubbes,

Anatomie of Abuses (ed. Furnivall, ii. p. 50). Barbers
'have also other kinds of cuts innumerable; and therefore when you come to be trimmed they will ask you
whether you will be cut to look terrible to your enemy
or amiable to your friend, grim and stern in countenance, or pleasant and demure.'

93. *make* (Pope) Q. 'maketh'

94. *supposèd fairness* i.e. the specious beauty created
by cosmetics.

97. *guilèd* v. G.

99. *Veiling an Indian beauty* Much annotated and
possibly corrupt; but if emphasis be laid on the word
'Indian,' and the Elizabethan horror of dusky skins
be borne in mind, does the passage present any real
difficulty?

101. *Therefore, thou* (Q. 1619) Q. 'Therefore then
thou' The misprint and the correction have been left
side by side.

106. *plainness* (Warburton) Q. 'palenes' The
emendation is generally accepted, since (i) silver has
just been rejected as a 'pale and common drudge,'
(ii) 'plainness' and not 'paleness' is the natural anti-
thesis to 'eloquence.' But it is not easy to explain the
error; Dr W. W. Greg suggests (privately) that possibly
'plaines' was accidentally misprinted 'palines' and was
then wrongly corrected.

109. *despair,* Q. 'deſpaire:' 110. *jealousy...* Q.
'iealouſie.' It looks as though the punctuation of the
copy has been transposed and the comma changed to
a period. Cf. p. 122.

112. *rain* Q. 'raine' Many edd. prefer 'rein,' of
which 'raine' was a common spelling. If Shakespeare
meant 'rein' then 'in measure' must be taken as an
expression from the manage (cf. note 2. 6. 10–11).

117. *whether* Q. 'whither'

122. *t'entrap* Q. 'tyntrap'

126. *unfurnished* v. G.

131–38. Q. prints this in italics. Cf. pp. 96–9.

132. *Chance as fair*... i.e. may you always have such good fortune... [1962].

134. *new*. So Q.

140. *I come by note, to give and to receive* Here Rowe, followed by most mod. edd., adds a S.D. 'kissing her.' But (i) Q. prints a comma at the end of the line, and therefore allows no time for the kiss, (ii) so far from giving Portia the kiss enjoined by the 'note,' Bassanio at l. 147 is still 'doubtful' until the note be 'confirmed, signed, ratified' by Portia. What happens, we think, is that Bassanio turns to Portia with the full intention of taking his kiss; but, after speaking ll 139–140 in a confident tone, he falters and kisses are not actually exchanged until l. 166 (v. note).

142. *eyes*, Q. 'eyes:'

155. *More rich* A broken line, printed with l. 156 by Q. There is almost certainly a 'cut' here. Note that while Portia has spoken of 'beauties' and 'livings,' she has said nothing of 'virtues' or 'friends.'

159. *Is some of something*... (Warburton) Q. 'fume of fomething:' F. 'fum of nothing' Most edd. read 'sum of something,' The passage has puzzled many, but if we read 'some' for 'fume' (the two words were not differentiated at this period) all seems clear. Portia is quibbling—her sum total is the portion of a portion (cf. N.E.D. 'something' 2), i.e. something very small. The Q. colon marks a natural pause.

162. *But she may learn* etc. A short line. Possibly the word 'still' has been omitted after 'happier.'

166. *her king*.... The Q. periods here and at 'converted' (l. 168) mark pauses for the lovers' kisses which naturally follow Portia's declaration of self-surrender.

170. *even now, but now* i.e. at this very instant.

172. *my lord's* Q. 'my Lords' Q. 1619, F. and all mod. edd. read 'my lord' The original reading underlines Portia's act of fealty.

179. *some oration fairly spoke* Is Shakespeare referring to some public speech by the Queen, or by Henry of Navarre at his coronation in 1594 (cf. note ll. 49–50 above)?

181. *multitude*, Q. 'multitude.'

191–92. *I wish you a...wish none from me* Gratiano is roguish as usual: he wishes them everything they can wish, so long (he hints) as their wishes do not clash with his own, and these, as he proceeds to explain, concern Nerissa.

194. *faith*, Q. 'fayth:'

200. *You loved, I loved—for intermission* (Theobald and edd.) Q. 'You lou'd, I lou'd for intermiſſion.' *for intermission...you* = for I don't let the grass grow under my feet any more than you do. v. G. 'intermission.'

204. *again*, v. G.

205. *roof* (Q. 1619) Q. 'rough'—which N.E.D. quotes as a 16th. cent: spelling.

214–18. *We'll play...stake down* It is significant that this piece of ribaldry should be a prose-patch in the midst of verse. It is, we think, certainly an 'addition,' and those who feel it unworthy of Shakespeare are at liberty, in a text like this, to regard it as actor's gag. Cf. p. 107.

218. S.D. Q. 'Enter Lorenzo, Ieſſica, and Salerio a meſſenger from Venice.'—after l. 220. F. omits 'a meſſenger from Venice.' For 'Salerio a meſſenger from Venice' cf. pp. 101–102.

219. *Lorenzo and his infidel* Theobald remarks the strange fact that Bassanio and Portia take no notice at all of Jessica's arrival, even though she contributes to the dialogue at ll. 285–91, and we may add that this one speech of hers, as we shall find, was probably intended to be deleted. The best explanation seems to be that Shakespeare, in revising, overlooked the necessity of a formal exchange of greetings between Portia and the Jewess. He did not entirely forget Jessica's presence, as l. 238 shows.

225–26. *So do I...welcome.* Q. prints this as one line. Possibly the special greeting to Jessica originally took place here. Note (i) l. 226 is broken, and (ii) Lorenzo (on the face of it rather rudely) ignores Portia's welcome.

237. *Will show you his estate* broken line.

S.D. Q. 'open the letter.' Cf. p. 105. Q. 1619 'He opens the Letter.' F. 'Opens the Letter.'

243. *fleece that he hath lost* Daniel suggests that Salerio is quibbling upon 'fleets'

244–45. *contents...steals* 'contents' is often singular in Shakespeare; cf. *Meas.* 4. 2. 193; *L.L.L.* 5. 2. 514. Or possibly 'paper' is the antecedent to 'that'

248. *constant* v. G.

250. *freely* Pope, following Q3, omitted this word, which is unnecessary either to the sense or the metre. If it be an interpolation, it probably comes from the theatre. There is an ugly repetition of the word at l. 255, whence perhaps the player inadvertently borrowed it.

272. *lord.* So Q.   277. *man.* So Q.

279. *impeach the freedom of the state* Cf. pp. 113–14 and 3. 3. 26–31; 4. 1. 38–9.

280. *justice.* So Q.

285–91. *When I was with him* etc. We are tempted to put this speech into square brackets as one from the old play which Shakespeare inadvertently left undeleted in the manuscript. Note (i) it jars upon a nerve which Shakespeare of all writers was generally most careful to avoid: that a daughter should thus volunteer evidence against her father is hideous; (ii) the others pay so little attention to what Jessica says that within a few lines Portia is urging Bassanio to adopt the course which the Jewess has just declared quite useless; (iii) the speech could be omitted without any loss to the context.

286. *Tubal...Chus* For these names v. Gen. x. 2, 6. Chus is not mentioned elsewhere in the text; possibly he actually appeared in the old play.

298–300. *What sum...deface the bond*　How much easier this would run:

> *Port.* What sum owes he the Jew?
> *Bass.*　　　　　　　　　　　Three thousand ducats.
> *Port.* Pay him six thousand and deface the bond.

The words 'For me' and 'What, no more?' are just the kind of small accretions that might creep into a player's part (cf. pp. 106–107) on the stage, though it is not easy to see how they got into the written 'parts.'

303. *thorough* (Steevens)　Q. 'through'

308. *over.*　So Q.

316–22.　Q. prints the letter in italics and omits the speech-heading. Cf. pp. 96–9.

327.　S.D. Q. 'Exeunt.'

3. 3.

S.D. Q. 'Enter the Iew, and Salerio, and Anthonio, and the Iaylor,' The three-fold 'and' reminds one of the *M.N.D.* text (cf. *M.N.D.* 1. 1. 19 note), and is here, as there, probably due to the compositor. For 'Salerio' v. pp. 101–103. Q. heads his speeches in the scene 'Sol.' and 'Sal.'; Q. 1619 alters 'Salerio' to 'Salarino' and F to 'Solanio.' Practically all mod. edd. follow Q 1619

We gather in the course of the scene that Antonio, under guard, has just paid a visit to Shylock to make some request or other, but we are not told the nature of the request, though l. 20 suggests that he had been praying for mercy. If so, we suspect that the scene has been abridged in order to cut out these 'bootless prayers, which would ill sort with the character of Antonio as Shakespeare conceived it. We feel practically certain that the whole scene as it stands belongs to the old play cf. pp. 109–12

2. *gratis.* So Q.　13. *more* So Q.　20 *prayers* So Q

11. short line, but no sign of a 'cut.'

17　S.D. Q. 'Exit Iew.'

24–5. Q. divides: 'I am sure...grant/this...to hold.'
26–31. *The duke cannot* etc. Cf. pp. 113–14.
36. S.D. Q. 'Exeunt.'

3. 4.

S.D. Q. 'Enter Portia, Nerriſſa, Lorenzo, Ieſſica, and a man of Portias.' It appears from ll. 45, 56 that the 'man's' name is Balthazar; cf. p. 100.

This scene must be supposed to take place on the same day as 3. 2. though at a later hour. Portia has had time to get married, to bid farewell to Bassanio and to make her arrangements for departure. There is great haste, as the trial is to begin 'to-morrow' (cf. 3. 3. 34).

1–21. We find it difficult to believe that this insipid dialogue is Shakespeare's.

2–3. *You have...a true conceit of god-like amity* Lorenzo and Portia have evidently been discussing, in Renaissance fashion, the relations between Love and Friendship (cf. note 1. 1. 1), and Friendship seems to have won the honours. No one has apparently noticed this hitherto, probably because Shakespeare did not intend them to do so. We fancy, in short, that the discussion was once given in full, but 'cut' in the revision, when the 'god-like amity' motive was suppressed throughout the play.

4. *lord.* So Q.   18. *lord.* So Q.
20. *soul* Q. 'ſoule;' 21. *cruelty?* Q. 'cruelty,'— transposed pointing.

22–3. *This comes too near...other things* Note the abrupt but characteristic Shakespearian turn to the conversation. It seems possible that at this point he found the verse of the original too tiresome, and so began composing himself.

23. *hear* Q. 'heere'
31. *monastery* Q. 'Monaſtry'—probably a copyist's error.
44. S.D. Q. 'Exeunt.'

45. *Now, Balthazar* This broken line, which Q. prints with l. 46, certainly denotes adaptation of some kind. For 'Balthazar' cf. p. 100.

46. *honest-true* (Walker) Q. 'honeſt true'

49. *Padua* (Theobald) Q. 'Mantua' Cf. 4. 1. 109, 399; 5. 1. 269. The university of Padua was the home of Civil Law in Italy. The 'Mantua' was probably a slip on Shakespeare's part. Cf. *Two Gent.* 2. 5. 1 (note), where 'Padua' is printed for 'Milan'

50. *cousin's hand* (Q. 1619) Q. 'coſin hands'

52. *imagined* i.e. with the speed of imagination. Cf. *Hen. V*, 3. chor. 1.

53. *tranect* Rowe reads 'traject' N.E.D. gives 'Tranect. Known only in the passage quoted, and prob. only a misreading or misprint of traiect (traject), in It. *traghetto* a ferry.' A compositor or transcriber might very easily misread *ai* as *an*; v. T.I. p. xli and Sh.Hand, p. 118.

56. S.D. Q. gives no 'exit.' Q. 1619 supplies one.

71. *died—* Q. 'dyed.'

72. *I could not do withal!* An indelicate allusion to ll. 61–2. Cf. A. H. Bullen, *Middleton's Works*, v. p. 30. [1952]

78. *turn to men* v. G.

79. broken line; but no metrical break.

80. *near* Q. 'nere'   81. *my* Q. 'my my'

84. S.D. Q. 'Exeunt.'

3. 5.

S.D. Q. 'Enter Clowne and Ieſſica.' For this scene, which we attribute to a playhouse adapter, v. pp. 107–108.

4. *agitation* Possibly a blunder for 'cogitation' (Eccles).

17. *I shall be saved by my husband* Henley quotes 1 Cor. vii. 14 'The unbelieving wife is sanctified by the husband.'

20. *e'en* (Q. 1619) Q. 'in' The same error is to be found in *Errors*, 2. 2. 101 (v. note), and we there explained it as a mishearing. The form does not appear in N.E.D. Cf. p. 103 note.

23. S.D. Q. 'Enter Lorenzo.'

25. *comes* (Q. 1619) Q. 'come'

34–9. *I shall answer that better* etc. Cf. pp. 107–108. Who was the black woman referred to in this passage? Clearly she has nothing to do with the play as it stands. Was she a character in an earlier version, e.g. a member of Morocco's train? Or was she some real figure, a London notoriety familiar to the audience for whom this dialogue was written? Holding the opinion we do on the authorship of this scene, we are inclined to interpret the reference as a topical one.

45. *Goodly Lord* This expletive, apparently not found elsewhere, is unnoted by N.E.D., which however quotes the 18th cent. expression 'goodly and gracious.' v. G. 'goodly.'

46. *then* Q. 'than' Cf. note 1. 2. 43.

47. *only 'cover' is the word* i.e. there is nothing more to do except to lay the cloth. At l. 50 Lancelot, of course, takes 'cover' in the sense of 'put on one's hat,' an action, he protests, that he is not so rude as to perform while speaking with Lorenzo and Jessica.

59. S.D. Q. 'Exit Clowne.'

60–5. *O dear discretion...Defy the matter* i.e. Lancelot's words are matched (suited) to their meaning with great discrimination (discretion), while other fools, that stand higher in (? court) favour, sacrifice the sense to mere word-play. This reads remarkably like a compliment to Kempe, who presumably impersonated Lancelot. If so, we believe that (i) 'A many fools that stand in better place' may refer to a rival comic player, (ii) some if not all of the preceding dialogue was of Kempe's own composition, and (iii) Shakespeare is unlikely to have penned such a compliment, partly because it is in bad

taste and partly because the verse in this scene is not
characteristic of him.

72–3. *merit it,/In reason* (Pope) Q. 'meane it, it/in
reaſon' Q. 1619 'meane it, then/In reaſon' F. 'meane
it, it/Is reaſon' The readings of Q. 1619 and F. are
both attempts at emendation and are of course mere
guesses. Most edd. have followed Q. 1619, which until
recently has been taken as the *editio princeps*. Pope's
reading makes good sense, involves no more alteration
than Q. 1619, and is palaeographically simple, 'merryt'
being taken for 'mean yt.' For a highly ingenious,
though we fear misguided, attempt to justify the Q. 1619
reading v. E. E. Kellett, *Suggestions*, pp. 16–20.

76. *one*, Q. 'one:'

84. *howsome'er* This form recurs in *Ham*. 1. 5. 84,
and *All's Well*, 1. 3. 57.

85. *set you forth* v. G. 'set forth.'

S.D. Q. 'Exit.'

4. 1.

S.D. Q. 'Enter the Duke, the Magnificoes, Anthonio,
Baſſanio, and Gratiano.' For 'magnificoes' v. G.
Charles Kean arranged this scene with a Doge, attended by six senators in red, his authority being a
picture at Hampton Court representing the state re-
ception by the Doge of Sir Henry Wotton, ambassador
of James I. Apparently no Doge had actually presided
over a court of justice in Venice since the middle of
the 14th cent., while Shakespeare was also incorrect
in introducing the senators as judges. On the other
hand, the arrangement of the scene corresponds very
closely with that at the trial of Lopez at the Guildhall,
the Earl of Essex presiding and the 'magnificoes' being
the city fathers; cf. pp. 116–18.

15. *He is ready* etc. Q. heads this, and the speech at
l. 107, with the prefix 'Salerio.' Cf. pp. 101–104. As it
is Solanio, and not Salerio, who stays behind in Venice

with Antonio, we give the speeches to him, though the absence of any entry for him at the head of the scene suggests that Shakespeare may have intended the lines for an 'attendant' merely. Both speeches concern the door of the court, which would naturally be guarded by an armed man.

16. S.D. Q. 'Enter Shylock.'—at l. 15. Q.'s prefixes for his speeches in this scene run as follows: ll. 35, 65, 67, 69, 85, 89, 122, 127, 139, 173 (Iewe); 180, 203, 220, 223, 225, 232, 243 (Shy.); 247, 249, 253, 256, 259, 292, 298, 301 (Iew); 311 (Shy.); 315 (Iew); and then 'Shy.' for the rest of the scene. Cf. p. 95.

20. *Thou'lt* Q. 'thowlt'

22. *exacts* Shakespearian 2nd pers. sing. Cf. *Meas.* 3. 1. 20.

25. *love,* Q. 'loue:' 26. *principal;* Q. 'principall,'—transposed pointing.

28. *back;* Q. 'backe,' 29. *down,* Q. 'downe;'—transposed pointing.

30. *his state* (Q. 1619; F.) Q. 'this ſtates'

31. *flint* (Q. 1619) Q. 'flints'

34. *gentle* 'A pun on Gentile is doubtless here intended' (Aldis Wright); cf. note 2. 6. 51.

36. *Sabbath* (Q. 1619; F.) Q. 'Sabaoth' which N.E.D. notes as a frequent spelling from 14th to 18th cent. Johnson treated 'Sabbath' and 'Sabaoth' as identical in the first edition of his dictionary, while even Sir Walter Scott confused the two.

39. *your charter and your city's freedom* Cf. pp. 113–14.

42–3. *I'll not answer...is it answered?* This has been often misinterpreted. Shylock refuses to give a direct answer; 'but suppose,' he says, 'it is just my humour—wouldn't that serve for an answer?' We of course follow the Q. punctuation.

47. *a gaping pig* Cf. G. 'gaping pig.'

49. *when the bag-pipe sings* etc. Scaliger relates a

story of one similarly affected by the lyre, which story was repeated in a translation from the French of Le Loier's *Treatise of Spectres* (1605), with the marginal note, 'Another Gentleman of this quality liued of late in Deuon neere Excester, who could not endure the playing on a Bagpipe' (sig. I 4 r.). Malone remarks that the story 'might have been current in conversation before [i.e. before 1605], or it may have found its way into some other book of the age.'

50–1. *urine: for affection,/Mistress of passion* (Cap. after Thirlby) Q. 'vrine for affection./Maisters of passion'. 'Mistress' and 'Masters' could both be contracted as 'Mrs'. Cf. the reverse misprint in *Shrew*, 1. 2. 18. For Q.'s missing colon v. p. 95, and for 'affection' and 'passion' v. G. Steevens quotes from Greene, *Never too Late*, 'His heart was fuller of passions than his eyes of affections.' [1952.]

56. *woollen* Dr Johnson had 'never seen a woollen bagpipe,' and so suggested 'wooden,' wood being the substance of which the pipe was made. Steevens read 'swollen', and Capel conjectured 'wawling', of which the Cambridge edd. of 1863 approved. The text is, nevertheless, undoubtedly correct: the 'bags' are quite commonly wrapped in baize or flannel.

62. *A losing suit* Shylock stands to lose three thousand ducats in exchange for 'A weight of carrion flesh.'

68. *offence* v. G.

71–2. *You may as well* etc. In some copies of Q. the words 'You may as' and 'Why he hath made' are omitted, having clearly dropped from the chase while the sheets were passing through the press. It was from one of these copies that the F. was printed, and this text reads accordingly 'Or euen as well vse queſtion with the Wolfe,/The Ewe bleate for the Lambe'

74. *bleat* (F.) Q. 'bleake'

75. *mountain pines* (F.) Q. 'mountaine of Pines'

100. *'tis mine* (Q. 1619; F.) Q. 'as mine' The

letters *ti* might conceivably be misread as an open *a*
with an initial overhead stroke (cf. Sh.Hand, plate v).
It is surprising that no one has defended the Q. reading;
possibly Shakespeare wrote 'is mine'

105—106. *Bellario…Whom I have sent for* Dr Johnson remarks: 'The Doctor and Court are here somewhat unskilfully brought together. That the Duke
would, on such an occasion, consult a Doctor of great
reputation, is not unlikely, but how should this be fore-
known by Portia?' One reply is that Shakespeare did
not write for Dr Johnson the editor but for an audience
in a theatre, which would be most unlikely to ask such
questions. On the other hand, the whole Bellario
business is left very obscure, e.g. was it Portia's intention from the beginning to act as judge, or did she
decide to assume the part when she heard her cousin
was ill? It seems possible, therefore, that the old play
had a Bellario scene of some kind, or at least a 'tranect'
scene at which news of Bellario's illness was brought to
Portia. Cf. note l. 152 below.

107. *My lord* etc. Q. gives this to 'Salerio'; cf. note
l. 15 above.

113. S.D. Furness quotes Booth's comment here:
'Shylock smiles scornfully [at Antonio's words] and
slowly drawing his knife at l. 118, kneels to whet it.'
We are inclined to think that Bassanio's words at
ll. 112—13 would be more likely to suggest the knife
to Shylock.

118. S.D. Q. 'Enter Nerriffa'

120. *my lord* Q. 'my L.'

123. *thy sole, but on thy soul* (Hanmer) Q. 'thy
foule: but on thy foule'

127. *No, none…to make* Shylock's brief, offhand,
contemptuous replies to Gratiano's torrential utterances
are very effective.

128. *inexorable* (F3) Q. 'inexecrable' Most edd.
follow F3, though some have supposed 'inexecrable' to

be an intensive form of 'execrable.' It is significant that the only other instance of 'inexecrable' that N.E.D. gives is 'a misprint for inexorable' from Constable's *Diana*, 1594.

129. *And for thy life* i.e. and for the continued existence of so foul a monster.

133–38. *thy currish spirit* etc. Cf. pp. 117–18.

134. *Wolf* Q. 'Woolfe' Q. also prints this word with a capital at l. 73.

136. *dam*, Q. 'dam;'

150–63. Q. gives no speech-heading for this letter; cf. pp. 96–9.

152. *in loving visitation...with me* This visit can never have taken place, since Portia was still at Belmont the day before the trial, whence she sends Balthazar to Padua for certain notes and garments which he is to bring to a rendezvous near Venice. Are we to suppose that this letter has been concocted by Portia? Cf. note ll. 105–106 above.

164. S.D. Q. 'Enter Portia for Balthazer'—after l. 163.

179. *Then must the Jew be merciful* Here 'must' carries the sense of inevitableness not of compulsion, i.e. the Jew will of course be merciful.

181. *strained* This, which means 'forced,' 'constrained,' is the emphatic word, being a comment upon Shylock's talk of 'compulsion.'

181–99. *The quality of mercy* etc. It was apparently Blackstone who first noticed that this speech, though addressed to a Jew, draws its chief arguments from the Lord's Prayer and the Christian doctrine of salvation (ll. 195–99). It is not sufficient to reply, as critics have done, that the Lord's Prayer is based upon earlier Hebrew prayers and that even the doctrine of salvation would appeal to a Jew, since it is exceedingly unlikely that these facts, known to modern biblical students, would be familiar to or even suspected by

Shakespeare. We are left, therefore, with two alternatives: either (i) he carelessly forgot for the moment that Shylock was a Jew, or (ii) that he quite deliberately made use of Christian arguments. And if the circumstances in which he first handled the play be remembered (cf. pp. 116–19), it is possible to suggest a reason which might prompt him to make Portia speak 'a little out of character.' A wretched old man was on trial for his life, and presiding over the trial was the great Earl of Essex, bosom friend of Southampton. It is even conceivable that Lopez was guiltless of the charges made against him; but Essex bore him a grudge and was determined to satisfy it. Thus it is possible that in giving Portia a speech addressed to a Jew on behalf of a Christian, Shakespeare was in reality addressing the Christians, and especially the presiding 'Duke,' on behalf of a poor old Jew. Certainly the references to crowns, sceptres and thrones, which are pointless in an appeal to Shylock, would have sounded gratefully enough in the ears of the Queen's favourite.

'If the voice of Shakespeare as prompter is ever to be heard in all his plays, it is to be heard in the wonderful pleading for mercy by Portia in *The Merchant of Venice* and by Isabella in *Measure for Measure*' (2. 2. 72–9), wrote the late Sir Walter Raleigh (Sh. Eng. i. 44–5). It should be added that both speeches are directly or indirectly derived from Seneca *De Clementia*, Bk i. 19 (v. letter by Prof. Sonnenschein, *Times Literary Supplement*, 16 Sept. 1904).

182. *as the gentle rain* Edd. quote *Ecclesiasticus* xxxv. 20 'Mercy is seasonable in the time of affliction, as clouds of rain in the time of drouth.'

183. *blessed* i.e. full of blessings; cf. 'guiled' G.

203. *My deeds* Shylock echoes 'The deeds of mercy' l. 199.

211. *bears down truth* 'oppresses honesty' (Dr Johnson).

218. *error* i.e. political not moral error, a departure from constitutional practice.

220. *A Daniel come to judgement* Though commentators have seen a reference here to the *History of Susanna* none appears to have observed the peculiar aptness of Shylock's comparison. Portia, the 'wise young judge,' so 'much more elder' than her looks, seated with the grave Venetian magnificoes, would seem to the Jew exactly analogous to the 'young youth whose name was Daniel' whom the elders of Israel summoned with the words, 'Come, sit down among us, and shew it us, seeing God hath given thee the honour of an elder' (*Sus.* 45, 50). The comparison, further, is eagerly and appropriately recalled by Gratiano later, when Portia saves Antonio from the cruel Shylock by much the same kind of verbal jugglery as that which saves Susanna from the wicked elders.

241. *then* Q. 'than' Cf. note 1. 2. 43.

253. *The flesh* Q. prints this with l. 252.

264–69. *For herein Fortune* etc. Cf. *Meas.* 3. 1. 6–41.

274. *Whether Bassanio...a love* Cf. note 1. 1. 1. Bassanio's protestation below (ll. 279–84) likewise belongs to the 'god-like amity' motive.

282. *life.* So Q.   287. *whom* (F.) Q. 'who'

293. *Bárrabas* To be accented Bárrăbás, as in Marlowe's *Jew of Malta*.

298, 309. short lines.

310. Q. divides 'O vpright Iudge,/Marke Iew, o learned Iudge.' This is interesting, and may represent the original arrangement; if so then 'Thyself shalt see the act' should stand as the broken line. There has probably been alteration of some kind here.

329. *A second Daniel* Cf. note l. 220 above.

358. *formerly* Q. 'formorly'

377. *To quit the fine* etc. i.e. I am content that he shall be forgiven even the fine which the duke has pro-

posed as a substitute for the half of his goods due to the
state (cf. ll. 357–58), provided etc.

379. *in use* Antonio will act as trustee for Lorenzo
and Jessica.

381. short line; a 'cut' may perhaps have occurred
here.

383. *become a Christian* It must be remembered
that Shakespeare's audience would see no wrong to
Shylock in this stipulation, but rather an enforced
benefit; Antonio's 'mercy' is such as Portia would
approve of.

394. *In christ'ning* etc. Q. gives this to 'Shy.' Both
Q. 1619 and F. restore it to 'Gra.'

396. S.D. Q. 'Exit.'

403. S.D. Q. 'Exit Duke and his traine.'

419. *as a fee* (Q. 1619) Q. 'as fee'

422. *Give me your gloves* The gloves are asked for in
order that the ring may be exposed to view.

423. *for your love* The reader should not miss the
comic irony of this.

444. S.D. Q. 'Exeunt.'

447. *wife's* Q. 'wiues'

450. S.D. Q. 'Exit Gratiano.'

453. S.D. Q. 'Exeunt.'

4. 2.

S.D. Q. 'Enter Nerriffa.' N.B. no entry given for
Portia; F. supplies one.

This scene follows immediately upon 4. 1. and obviously takes place just outside the court-house.

4. S.D. Q. 'Enter Gratiano.'

5. a prose line; clearly, we think, a piece of
textual stitching.

15. *old swearing* v. G. 'old.'

19. *you* Q. 'yov'

S.D. Q. gives no 'exeunt.'

5. 1.

S.D. Q. 'Enter Lorenzo and Ieffica.'

Capell heads this scene 'Belmont. Avenue to Portia's house.' It is clear from the frequent references to moon, stars and darkness (ll. 1, 25, 55, 59–60, 93, 110–14, 125–27, 143, 221) that the moon shines brightly but fitfully, and the reader must imagine it peeping in and out of 'lazy-pacing clouds' as the scene goes forward.

1–22. *In such a night* etc. Hunter first drew attention to Shakespeare's debt to Chaucer in this lovely passage.

2–6. *When the sweet wind...Cressid lay that night.* Cf. Chaucer, *Troilus and Criseyde*, 647–79.

7–8. *Thisbe...lion's shadow* Cf. Chaucer, *Legend of Good Women* (Thisbe), 796–812. The 'dew' was no doubt suggested to Shakespeare by ll. 774–75 which tell of a meeting between the lovers when

> Aurora with the stremes of hir hete
> Had dryed up the dew of herbes wete.

10–12. *Stood Dido...again to Carthage* Malone noted that Shakespeare has here transferred to Dido the picture Chaucer gives of Ariadne. Cf. *Legend*, 2189–2206.

13–14. *Medea...old Æson* Shakespeare found the name of Medea in the *Legend*, but it seems only to have reminded him of Ovid, for he owes these lines to suggestions in Golding's trans. of *The Metamorphoses* (vii. 162 et seq.).

24. S.D. Q. 'Enter a Meffenger.' His name is given at ll. 28, 52, but his speeches are headed 'Meff.' Cf. p. 100.

33. *a holy hermit* 'I do not perceive the use of this hermit, of whom nothing is seen or heard afterwards,' wrote Johnson, 'the Poet had first planned his fable some other way, and inadvertently when he changed his scheme, retained something of its original design.'

But cf. the 'secret vow' described at 3. 4. 27–32, and Stephano's words about Portia's devotions at ll. 30–2 just above. I owe this note to a private letter by Mr R. H. Truell.

38. S.D. Q. 'Enter Clowne.'

39–49. *Sola, sola* etc. Cf. pp. 105–107. 'Lancelot is imitating the horn of the courier or post as he was called, who always wore that appendage suspended from his neck' (Staunton). Cf. Launce's 'So-ho' *Two Gent*. 3. 1. 189.

42. *Master Lorenzo? Master Lorenzo* (Aldis Wright) Q. 'M. Lorenzo & M. Lorenzo' Many edd. read 'Master Lorenzo and Mistress Lorenzo' but, as Wright points out, Lancelot says 'Tell him,' not 'Tell them,' at l. 47. Furness suggests that the Q. ampersand was a misprint for an interrogation mark.

50. *Sweet soul* These words are misplaced in Q. and printed at the end of Lancelot's speech (l. 49). Cf. pp. 105–107. *coming.* So Q.

52. *Stephano* (Q. 1619) Q. 'Stephen'—possibly a compositor's expansion of 'Steph.' in the copy.

54. *your music* Lorenzo, himself a guest, thus speaks of the 'music of the house' (cf. l. 99) to one of Portia's servants.

57. *ears—soft* Q. 'eares soft'

58. *touches* v. G.

60. *patens* Q. 'pattens' Malone read 'patine' and many edd. follow. For 'paten' v. G. Dyce aptly quotes from Sylvester's *Du Bartas*: 'Th' Almighties finger fixed many a million/Of golden scutchions ['platines dorées'] in that rich pavillion,' and 'That sumptuous canapy,/The which th'un-niggard hand of Majesty/Poudred so thick with shields so shining cleer' (The Fourth Day of the First Week, ed. 1641, pp. 33, 34). We seem to hear an even more direct echo of Du Bartas in 'this most excellent canopy...this majestical roof fretted with golden fire' (*Ham.* 2. 2. 311–14). It

has been objected that to liken the points of silver light in the night sky to golden plates is absurd; but the Elizabethan imagination was guided by the old astronomy, which conceived of the stars as large round bright objects literally 'inlaid' in their appropriate spheres; v. next note.

61–66. *There's not the smallest orb...we cannot hear it* A reference to 'the music of the spheres.' The idea was of course a commonplace, but the expression of it in Florio's Montaigne (*Of Custom*, bk. i. ch. 22) offers a remarkably close parallel. Speaking of 'how custome quaileth and weakeneth our customary senses' Montaigne refers to 'what Philosophers deeme of the celestiall musicke, which is that the bodies of it's circles, being solid smooth, and in their rowling motion, touching and rubbing one against another, must of necessitie produce a wonderfull harmonie: by the changes and entercaprings of which, the revolutions, motions, cadences, and carrols of the asters and planets, are caused and transported. But that universally the hearing senses of these low world's creatures, dizzied and lulled asleepe, as those of the Ægyptians are, by the continuation of that sound, how loud and great soever it be, cannot sensibly perceive or distinguish the same.' Florio's translation was first printed in 1603; but Florio was a member of Southampton's household for many years (v. Stopes, *Southampton*, p. 137), and Shakespeare may have read the early books of his Montaigne in manuscript.

63. *young-eyed* i.e. with sight ever-young; v. G.

64. *Such harmony* etc. We have added a note of exclamation to this line to bring out the meaning of the passage, which has been much misunderstood. The 'harmony' is still the 'music of the spheres' (not some inner harmony of the soul, as some have imagined), and the 'immortal souls' are 'the young-eyed cherubins,' who have this harmony in them (cf. 'The man that

hath no music in himself' l. 84) because they *hear* the music. We too have 'immortal souls,' but while they are grossly closed in by 'this muddy vesture of decay' (our bodies) we cannot hear like the cherubins. What a magnificent expansion this, of Florio's 'these low world's creatures, dizzied and lulled asleepe' (v. previous note)!

67. *wake Diana* i.e. not 'awaken,' but 'keep her vigil.' Cf. 'wake' *L.L.L.* G.

69. *And draw her* etc. Short line, but of course of no bibliographical significance.

S.D. Q. 'play Muſique.' Q. 1619 'Muſicke playes.' Cf. p. 105.

71. v. G. 'spirits,' 'attentive.' Cf. *Troil.* 1. 3. 251–52 'To awake his ear,/To set his sense on the attentive bent.'

72–80. *For do but note* etc. Cf. *Temp.* 4. 1. 175–78.

78. *mutual* v. G.

80. *the poet* Shakespeare's favourite Ovid, who tells the story in his *Metamorphoses* (bks. x, xi).

88. *Erebus* Q. 'Terebus' F. 'Erobus' The capitals E and T are not unlike in English script; v. Sh.Hand, plate vii.

89. S.D. Q. 'Enter Portia and Nerriſſa.'

93. *When the moon shone* It was shining at l. 67, but a cloud has meanwhile obscured it; cf. head-note.

99. *your music* i.e. your musicians.

100. *Nothing is good* etc. Cf. *Ham.* 2. 2. 255–57.

110. *the moon sleeps* etc. Shakespeare thus emphasises the darkness and so leads up to the dialogue that follows.

111. S.D. F. 'Muſicke ceaſes'

122. S.D. F. 'A Tucket ſounds.' v. G. 'tucket.' Verity writes: 'It seems as if formerly each person had his own trumpet-note like his private crest. Cf. *Lear*, 2. 4. 185–86 "*Cornwall*. What trumpet's that? *Regan*. I know't, my sister's".'

125–27. *This night...the sun is hid*. The moon is bright once more. Portia and Bassanio are to see each other face to face.

127. S.D. Q. 'Enter Baſſanio, Anthonio, Gratiano, and their followers.'

128–29. *We should hold day* etc. 'If you would always walk in the night, it would be day with us, as it is now on the other side of the world' (Malone).

137. *in all sense* v. G. 'sense.'

142. *this breathing courtesy* Cf. 'courteous breath' 2. 9. 90; 'the verbal complimentary form' (Malone).

149. *give to me* (Steevens) Q. 'giue me' Most edd. restore the rhythm by reading 'poesy' with Q. 1619. v. G. 'posy.'

151. *leave* v. G. Cf. ll. 173, 197.

157. *respective* v. G.   *kept it.* So Q.

170. *And riveted* (Pope) Q. 'And ſo riueted' Dyce notes, 'The "ſo" in this line was evidently repeated by mistake from the "ſo" just above it in the preceding line but one.' *flesh.* So Q.

176. *unkind cause* (Walker) Q. 'vnkind a cauſe'

194–203. The device of ending a number of consecutive lines with the same word was a not uncommon one with dramatists of the age. Walker cites *K. John*, 3. 1. 12–15; *R. III*, 1. 3. 292–94; *Errors*, 1. 2. 89–90. The effect here is to reassure the audience: Portia and Bassanio are obviously not serious.

206. *zeal*, Q. 'zeale:'

211. *a civil doctor* i.e. a doctor of civil law.

221. *candles of the night* Cf. 'Night's candles are burnt out' (*Rom.* 3. 5. 9); 'There's husbandry in heaven; Their candles are all out' (*Macb.* 2. 1. 5); 'those gold candles fixed in heaven's air' (*Son.* 21).

230. *it.* So Q.   231. *home.* So Q.

250. *for his wealth* i.e. for his advantage; to obtain his happiness (Johnson). Steevens quotes the *Litany*: 'In all time of our tribulation; in all time of our wealth.'

252. *miscarried.* So Q.

263. *In lieu of this* v. G. 'lieu.'

279–80. *You shall not know...this letter.* This beauti-ful example of Shakespeare's dramatic impudence has been severely criticised by some pundits. A more painstaking dramatist, no doubt, would have brought on the letter by a solaing 'post' (cf. note ll. 39–49 above), and thus ruined entirely the stillness and intimacy of this wonderful finale.

295. *you drop manna* etc. Lorenzo and Jessica had run through their money in Genoa; cf. 3. 1. 101–102.

298. *full.* So Q.

299. *And charge us...inter'gatories* This is Portia's last little piece of law jargon; v. G. 'inter'gatory.'

inter'gatories Q. 'intergotories'

301. *inter'gatory* Q. 'intergory'

308. S.D. Q. 'Exeunt.'

A NOTE ON THE TEXTS OF
1619 AND 1623

The connexion between the 1600 and 1619 Quartos is thus defined in Mr A. W. Pollard's *Shakespeare Folios and Quartos* (p. 98): 'The view of the Cambridge editors is that the two texts were independently set up from the same manuscript. But the use of capitals for the name of GOD in the same passage, and in that passage only (2. 2. 68), seems to prove that one printer must have copied the other. Roberts, like other printers of his day, used this typographical reverence in theological works, and a compositor accustomed to the practice followed it in a single, quite inappropriate, place. It is easier to believe that a second compositor imitated him mechanically than that both took it from a manuscript, where, indeed, it is hardly conceivable that it could have occurred.' If further evidence be required, it can be found in a dozen other typographical coincidences, in some fifteen common misprints, and in a number of common errors in punctuation. It is to be noted, moreover, that in many of these instances the F. text agrees with the two Quartos. A good example, which combines mispunctuation with misprint, occurs in 4. 1. 49–52, which apart from differences of spelling appears in all three texts as

> And others when the bag-pipe sings i'th' nose,
> Cannot contain their urine for affection.
> Masters of passion sways it to the mood
> Of what it likes or loathes, now for your answer:

Even more significant to our mind is the fact that Q. 1619 often agrees precisely with Q. 1600 in the arrangement of its stage-directions. For instance at 5. 1. 127, although there is plenty of room to print the whole direction in a single line, Q. 1600 gives us

> *Enter Baſſanio, Anthonio, Gratiano, and their*
> *followers.*

And both Q. 1619 and F. 1623 follow this arrangement exactly. Finally, seeing that we have found poverty in capitals to be the most striking typographical feature of the 1600 text (v. p. 94), we may expect to discover traces of this in the other two texts, if they are actually reprints of it. Nor are we disappointed. We may take two passages to illustrate the point:

(i) 4. 1. 241–42.

Q. 1600.   *Por.* Why than thus it is,
              you muſt prepare your boſome for his knife.

Q. 1619.   *Por.* Why then thus it is,
              You muſt prepare your boſome for his knife.

F. 1623.   *Por.* Why then thus it is:
              you muſt prepare your boſome for his knife.

(ii) 5. 1. 113–14.

Q. 1600.   *Por.* He knowes me as the blind man knowes the Cuckoe
              by the bad voyce?

Q. 1619.   *Por.* He knowes me as the blinde man knowes
              The Cucko, by the bad voyce.

F. 1623.   *Por.* He knowes me as the blinde man knowes the
              Cuckow by the bad voice?

The lower case 'y' with which Q. 1600 begins 4. 1. 242 has been inadvertently imitated by the F. compositor, though not it will be noticed by the compositor of 1619. In the passage from 5. 1., on the other hand, the lower case 'b' set up in 1600 has led both the later compositors to read the speech as prose, and each has adopted his own arrangement. These two speeches of Portia, in short, prove conclusively that both Q. 1619 and F. 1623 were set up from the Hayes Quarto of 1600.

Nevertheless either text differs from the 1600 Quarto in readings which no one could regard as due to the chance variations of compositors. Still more remarkable, both agree, as against the parent text, in a fashion which almost suggests some kind of common editorial supervision. Let us look at these matters in turn.

(*a*) *Variants in Q.* 1619. It is quite clear that the copy of Q. 1600 used by Jaggard's compositors in 1619 had first been looked over by some scribe who had freely made alterations therein. Thus in 2. 2. not only is the 'Iobbe' of Q. 1600 corrected to 'Gobbo,' but some of Lancelot's

blunders are likewise 'corrected.' The words 'deuill incarnation' (l. 25) are changed to 'diuell incarnall,' and
'confuſions' to 'concluſions' (l. 34), while the idea of a
fiend counselling 'well' is evidently taken as unseemly,
since the 'well' is altered to 'ill' (l. 20). An even more
elaborate emendation is to be found at 1. 3. 61-2, where in
place of the original 'is hee yet poſſeſt/How much ye
would?' Q. 1619 reads 'are you reſolued,/How much he
would haue?'—a change for which no compositor is likely
to have been responsible, though it is not at first obvious
for what purpose it was made. The passage in the original
is an aside to Bassanio, in the middle of a speech by Antonio
to Shylock, who hears the aside and replies to it. It is
therefore just a little awkward, and might be misunderstood
by a stupid editor. On the other hand, we feel, the awkwardness is even more likely to have struck players who had to
perform this particular scene. In other words, the reading
of Q. 1619, which directs the question to Shylock, is easier
to manage on the stage, though of course it ruins the verse.
This change, therefore, at least suggests the possibility that
the editorial scribe, whose presence is discernible in Q. 1619,
had some connexion with the playhouse.

Other 1619 variants seem to point in the same direction.
It is evident, for instance, that the scribe is interested in
entries and exits. Not only does he supply missing exits[1]
at 2. 3. 14; 3. 4. 56, but at 2. 2. 114 he adds 'Exit one of his
men,' while the curious and ambiguous 'his man that was
the Clowne' in the entry at the head of 2. 5. in Q. 1600 has
been altered to 'Lancelet.' Still more significant is the
editorial attempt to grapple with the 'Sal-Sol-Salerio'
problem (cf. pp. 100-104). Every 'Sol.', 'Sola.', 'Solanio'
in 1. 1.; 2. 4.; 2. 8.; and 3. 1. is carefully altered to 'Sal.' or its
equivalent, and at the head of 3. 3. 'Salarino' has been sub-
stituted for 'Salerio.' Further, the scribe has restored to
Gratiano a speech in 4. 1. which Q. 1600 had wrongly
ascribed to Shylock (v. note 4. 1. 394). Finally (a point
which would have delighted the late Mr Bayfield) there can
be little doubt that the 1619 editor favoured abbreviated
forms, since he has introduced quite a number into the

---

[1] Sometimes he is careless: at 1. 1. 72, for instance, he adds an
'exit' which is incorrect.

text, e.g. y'are 1. 1. 46; ile 1. 2. 94; ifaith 1. 3. 149; ha
2. 2. 156; lib'rall 2. 2. 182; diffrence 2. 5. 2; Ime 2. 8. 3;
on't 3. 1. 110. Of course, all these changes may have been
made by some scribe in Jaggard's office, but we cannot help
suspecting that the hand that made them belonged to a
man concerned with the correct distribution of players'
parts and with the proper delivery of 'lines'—in a word to
some kind of book-holder.

(b) *Variants in F.* Of the origin of the F. variants there
can at any rate be no doubt. The addition of the familiar
Flo. Cornets at the entries of Morocco (2. 7. head) and
Arragon (2. 9. 3) is conclusive proof of the book-holder's
hand, to say nothing of other musical jottings, such as *Here
Muſicke* (3. 2. 62), *Muſicke ceaſes* (5. 1. 111) and *A Tucket
ſounds* (5. 1. 122). Furthermore, the performance for which
these jottings were made was no doubt a Jacobean one,
seeing that the alteration of 'I pray God grant' to 'I wiſh'
(1. 2. 105) shows that the book-holder was conscious of the
necessity of keeping on the right side of the blasphemy
statute, while the significant substitution of 'other Lord'
for 'Scottish Lorde' (1. 2. 72) tells us a Stuart had succeeded
a Tudor. In the light of these facts, we do well to remind
ourselves that *The Merchant of Venice* was played on
'Shrousunday,' 1605, before King James, who was so
pleased thereat that it was performed two days later again
at his command (v. Chambers, *Eliz. Stage*, iv. 172).

(c) *Agreement between F. and Q.* 1619. The most
striking readings in which the 1619 and 1623 texts agree as
against the Hayes Quarto are the following: Slubber <
Slumber 2. 8. 39; goſſips report < goſſip report 3. 1. 6–7;
e'ne < in 3. 5. 20; his ſtate < this ſtates 4. 1. 30; *Gra.* <
Shy. 4. 1. 394; Poeſie < poſie 5. 1. 149, 152. There are
others, which might have been hit upon by two compositors
working independently. The six we have just cited, however, seem to demand the intervention of somebody outside
the printer's office. And if so then, while Q. 1619 and F.
1623 are independently printed from Q. 1600, they are
linked together in some way which those who are interested
in the 'copy' for the collected edition of 1619 would do well
to investigate[1]. All we need say here is that we can feel

[1] Dr W. W. Greg, who has read these notes in MS., agrees
that 'Q. 1619 was printed from a copy of Q. 1600 which had

confident that this link, whatever it may have been, had nothing to do with Shakespeare himself; for though 'slubber,' 'e'ne,' 'his ſtate,' and '*Gra*.' are genuine corrections, 'goſſips report' and 'Poeſie' belong to exactly the same class of stupid alteration which, as we have noted above, was characteristic of the 1619 editor.

undergone some revision—possibly not *ad hoc*' but thinks it 'most unlikely that in 1619 Jaggard should have had any access to playhouse MSS.' His tentative suggestion is that the copy of Q. 1600 (revised) from which Q. 1619 was printed may have been 'still in Jaggard's office in 1623' and have undergone 'further revision by collation with the playhouse copy and was then used as copy for F.'

THE STAGE-HISTORY OF
THE MERCHANT OF VENICE

Meres mentions *The Merchant of Venice* among Shakespeare's comedies. Henslowe's entry concerning a 'Venetian comedy' has been discussed elsewhere in this volume (p. 116). The title-page of the 'good' Quarto of 1600 presents the play 'as it hath beene diuers times acted by the Lord Chamberlaine his Seruants.' There is a tradition that Richard Burbadge was the first actor of Shylock and played the part in a red wig; but the evidence for it is confined to an elegy on Burbadge's death in a form of doubtful authenticity printed by Collier:

> the red-hair'd Jew
> Which sought the bankrupt merchant's pound of flesh
> By woman-lawyer caught in his own mesh.

The Merchant of Venice was acted by the King's company before the Court at Whitehall on Sunday, February 10, 1605, and again, by the King's command, on the following Tuesday, which was Shrove Tuesday.

After the Restoration it was one of the plays allotted to Killigrew in January, 1669. It had to wait long for a hearing. Yet in the early years of the eighteenth century Shylock was a well-known character. The place of *The Merchant of Venice* was taken by *The Jew of Venice*, an adaptation from Shakespeare's play by George Granville, later first Lord Lansdowne, which was first acted in 1701, probably in May, at the Lincoln's Inn Fields Theatre. Bassanio was played by Betterton; Shylock by Doggett; Antonio by Verbruggen; Gratiano by Booth; Lorenzo by Baily; Nerissa by Mrs Bowman; Jessica by Mrs Porter, and Portia by Mrs Bracegirdle. Both the Gobbos were cut out. Their humour was the less needed because Granville's Shylock was much more comical a part than Shakespeare's. Shylock is mentioned by Downes among Doggett's comic parts, and Doggett's being cast for it is enough to show that it was played as broadly comic. Granville's book, published in June, 1701, survives to prove it. Bevill Higgons, Esquire, wrote the prologue, which assures the audience that:

> The first rude Sketches *Shakespear's* Pencil drew,
> But all the shining Master-stroaks are new.

They included the rewriting of a good deal of Shakespeare, and the cutting of a good deal, and the interpolation of a scene between Shylock and Antonio in prison, of the banquet at Bassanio's, and (at any rate in the earliest performances) of a mask of Peleus and Thetis. *The Jew of Venice* was pretty frequent in the bills of Betterton's Lincoln's Inn Fields Theatre till 1731, and of Rich's Covent Garden in and after 1734. It occurs once or twice also at the Haymarket. On September 8, 1711, Pinkethman presented at Greenwich *The Jew of Venice or The Female Lawyer*, 'as it was perform'd before her Majesty on her Birthday at St. James's'—a performance of which I have found no other record; and on September 24, 1719, *The Jew of Venice* is played (possibly as a droll) for Harper's benefit at Bullock's Booth in Bird Cage Alley, Southwark fair. The Shylock at Southwark fair was Benjamin Griffin, a very popular comedian, who is first found playing the part at Lincoln's Inn Fields in May, 1717. His frequent performances certainly presented the character in the low comic vein, and probably with a comic nose. Among other Shylocks in this period we find Boheme, Ogden, Aston, and Arthur; and among the Portias are Mrs Bradshaw, Mrs Thurmond, Mrs Seymour, Mrs Berriman and Mrs Hallam. Mills and Ryan were the principal actors of Antonio.

On February 14, 1741, Drury Lane, which had not

previously staged *The Merchant of Venice* in any form, gave the famous production in which, on the initiative of Macklin, Shakespeare's play was restored to the theatre. Macklin had persuaded Fleetwood to let him act Shylock, and during rehearsals kept his idea of the part as secret as he could. On the night he appeared in a peaked beard, and wore a loose black gown and a three-cornered red hat, because he had learned that such was the prescribed dress of Jews in Italy. The Jew's private calamities, says Davies, made 'some tender impression on the audience,' which means that Shylock was no longer a low comedy part. Macklin made him malevolent, and of a forcible and terrifying ferocity He was 'slow, calm in his impenetrable cunning...unflinching even to the extreme of torture.' The performance made Macklin's reputation. The piece was played some twenty-one times in its first season, and Macklin's Shylock became as great a 'draw' as Garrick's Hamlet was later. It was accepted by its age as faithful to Shakespeare's intention; and Pope, asked at a party for an epitaph on Macklin, promptly gave:

> Here lies the Jew
> That Shakespeare drew.

Macklin went on playing Shylock pretty frequently for nearly 50 years. His last attempted appearance in the part was at Drury Lane on May 7, 1789, when he may have been 99 years of age. He broke down early in the performance, and Ryder finished it for him. His Shylock was accepted as Shakespeare's: his play also was Shakespeare's. The Gobbos are restored and so are 'Morochus' and Arragon. This, indeed, was one of the earliest efforts to play Shakespeare as it was written. The only survival of the Granville attitude to the play was the casting for Portia of Mrs Clive, an actress unsuited to the great lady of Belmont. In the trial-scene she used to give imitations of living judges and counsel.

At this famous performance of February 14, 1741, Antonio was played by Quin; Bassanio by Milward; Gratiano by Mills; Lorenzo by Havard; Lancelot Gobbo by Chapman; Old Gobbo by Johnson; Morocco by Cashel; Arragon by Turbutt; Tubal by Taswell; Nerissa by Mrs Pritchard, and Jessica by Mrs Woodman.

From that time onward *The Merchant of Venice* was in high favour, both at Drury Lane and at Covent Garden; and Foote gave it at the Haymarket. In January, 1742 (perhaps a little earlier), Arne wrote a song for Portia; and two songs were soon introduced for Lorenzo, which became a 'singing part' and was allotted to singers, like Lowe and, later, Beard. One of Lorenzo's songs was sung not inappropriately at Belmont in the fifth act; and one, very inappropriately, under Jessica's window just before the elopement. As the eighteenth century went on, there was a tendency to introduce more songs, and also dances and other diversions; and the playbills are careful to mention the Italian or other dancers who will appear. In May, 1754, for instance, Garrick's production at Drury Lane has Beard for Lorenzo: at the end of Act III a Pierrots' dance; in Act IV a dialogue called *Damon and Chloe* by Master Reinhold and Miss Thomas; and in Act V a hornpipe by Walker and others. But in the main Shakespeare's play was given as he wrote it. Garrick never acted in it at Drury Lane; but he chose it for the opening performance of the theatre under his management on September 15, 1747; and it was for this performance that Samuel Johnson wrote the famous prologue containing the lines:

> The drama's laws the drama's patrons give,
> For we that live to please, must please to live.

Between 1741 and 1784, when John Philip Kemble first essayed the part, the best Shylocks after Macklin were King and Henderson. Others were Shepherd,

Roscoe, Lalauze, Ryan, Yates, Arthur, Sheridan, Foote (in 1758, for his own benefit at Covent Garden), Shuter (apparently once only) and Palmer. In 1744, Mrs Woffington first appears at Drury Lane as Portia; in 1746, Mrs Pritchard at Covent Garden; in 1761, Miss Macklin, the actor's daughter, at Covent Garden; in 1768, Mrs Abington at Drury Lane; in 1775, on December 29, at Drury Lane, to the Shylock of King, 'a young lady, her first appearance'—a young lady later known to fame as Sarah Siddons. Of these the best appears to have been Mrs Woffington, whose Portia was said to be full of dignity, judgment and sensibility. There were many other Portias, including Mrs Vincent, Mrs Bland, Mrs Dancer, Mrs Yates, Mrs Bulkley, Mrs Barry and Ellen Tree. First Chapman, and after him Shuter, were favourites as Lancelot Gobbo.

In January, 1784, John Philip Kemble made his first appearance as Shylock at Drury Lane; and thereafter gradually replaced King in the part, although he was never very happy or successful in it. His Portia during the next twenty years was nearly always Mrs Siddons. Stephen Kemble once 'attempted' the part in December, 1802, with Mrs Powell for Portia and Suett for Old Gobbo; and he played it there again in 1813. At Covent Garden Macklin was still for a few years the principal Shylock; and Harley, Murray, Elliston, Rees and George Frederick Cooke were all seen in the part, Mrs Pope being the great Portia of the time, with Miss Younge, Miss de Camp, Miss Betterton, Miss Murray all trying it. At the Haymarket also the play was several times acted, with Williamson, Ryder and Palmer on different occasions as Shylock. In 1803, on November 19, another epoch in the stage-history of the play begins. John Philip Kemble gave his own production of it at Covent Garden. He himself chose to play Antonio, giving Shylock to Cooke and Bassanio to Charles Kemble. Mrs Siddons was Portia, Munden was

Lancelot Gobbo, and Emery Old Gobbo; and with Knight as Gratiano, Hill as Lorenzo, Miss St Leger as Nerissa and Mrs Creswell as Jessica, the play must have been finely acted. It still had the solos and duets for Lorenzo and 'Jessy,' as Shylock's daughter had come to be called; but the adventitious entertainments had been mainly shorn away, leaving room for some of Shakespeare's poetry in the fifth act, which had of late been crowded out. Cooke seems to have acted Shylock for the last time at Covent Garden in June, 1810; and in the winter of that year John Philip Kemble took up the part again. A general impression of all these Shylocks may be gained from Hazlitt, who, in his *Characters of Shakespear's Plays*, describes the 'caricature' which 'we had been used to see, a decrepid old man, bent with age and ugly with mental deformity, grinning with deadly malice, with the venom of his heart congealed in the expression of his countenance, sullen, morose, gloomy, inflexible, brooding over one idea, that of his hatred, and fixed on one unalterable purpose, that of his revenge.' Not altogether, one would say, an un-Shakespearian Shylock; but Hazlitt was not, perhaps, quite fair to Cooke and Kemble and Henderson and King, because he was flushed with his admiration of the Shylock of Edmund Kean.

Kean made his historic first appearance as Shylock at Drury Lane on January 26, 1814. The story is too well known to need telling here. Its principal elements are a shabby little strolling player, heart-sick at being kept hanging about by muddling managers, and despised by the Drury Lane company during the hurried and perfunctory rehearsal; a scrubby black wig in place of the traditional red; forebodings; a very small audience; a triumph; the intoxication of the town. More to the present purpose is it that Kean on that night gave London its first experience of romantic acting in full blast. Hazlitt, Talfourd, Lewes and other critics were loud in his praise; and, though during Kean's reign Terry, Warde, Yates, Young and Macready played the part, Kean's was the only Shylock. Curiosities of the period are the performances of Mr Sherenbeck, of Rochester, who at Covent Garden on July 9, 1817, played the part 'in the Jewish dialect' (at the Royal Victoria Hall, London, on April 23, 1924, Mr Swarz, a Jewish actor, played a portion of the part with a strong Jewish accent); of Wallack, who at Drury Lane on June 11, 1821, gave the trial-scene 'after the manner of Kean,' and of Miss Clara Fisher, who acted the part of Shylock at Bath and at Drury Lane in 1823. Kean's was a personal triumph, and his *Merchant of Venice* made no difference to the staging of the comedy as a whole. When Samuel Phelps chose the part of Shylock for his first appearance in London (at Benjamin Webster's Haymarket, August 28, 1837) the play, like Kemble's version, still lacked Morocco and Arragon. So did the version of Macready, who (having first acted Shylock at Covent Garden in 1823, with Miss Ogilvie for his Portia and Charles Kemble very good as Bassanio) staged the play very beautifully at Drury Lane in December, 1841, and cut out the unauthentic songs and duets.

The tendency of the nineteenth century was towards the elaborate and realistic mounting of the play. In 1848–49 Charles Kean produced it under Webster at the Haymarket; in 1858 at his Princess's Theatre he staged it even more realistically, with bridges, canals and gondolas. He transposed and altered the text, restored some of Morocco and Arragon, but cut out Lorenzo and Jessica at Belmont; and it was noted that he used no Jewish accent as Shylock. In his Venetian crowd there was a little girl carrying doves. Her name was Ellen Terry; and in April, 1875 (Hermann Vezin and Barry Sullivan had meanwhile both appeared as Shylock), the same Miss Ellen Terry gave at the Prince of Wales's Theatre a performance of Portia which was

one of the most beautiful of all her beautiful achieve-
ments. The play was produced by Mr and Mrs Bancroft. If theatre-goers' memories are to be trusted,
Miss Ellen Terry's Portia of 1875 was even more en-
trancing than her Portia at the Lyceum four years later.
The smallness of the stage of the Prince of Wales's
Theatre entailed in the Bancroft production some
transposition and compression of scenes, and songs from
other plays by Shakespeare were introduced. But the
alterations were not severe nor tasteless; and only the
failure of Charles Coghlan as Shylock, it is recorded,.
prevented the revival from being as successful as it
was good to look at. Henry Irving's Shylock (Lyceum
Theatre, November 1, 1879) was one of his greatest
parts. In his long brown gaberdine and his black cap
with a yellow line on it, this Shylock was the aristocrat
of an ancient race and religion, looking down with
malevolent dignity on the occidental upstarts. He was
usually calm and proud, but his rage and scorn would
break out in sudden transports. There was no Arragon
in Irving's version of the play; and the fifth act was a
good deal cut. The mounting was one of the Lyceum
Theatre's most beautiful.

The germ of the idea of a noble Shylock we probably owe to Macready. Since Irving, it has pretty well
held the field, modified by the personalities and ideas
of the various actors who have played the part. Notable
efforts at another sort of Shylock were seen in the Elizabethan Stage Society's production in 1898, when
Mr William Poel attempted to restore what is commonly
accepted as the Elizabethan tradition; and in a performance at the Royal Court Theatre in February, 1914,
when Mr Michael Sherbrooke contrived a remarkable
blend of the comical and the terrible. The popularity
of the play continues to be so great that it is impossible
to chronicle all its recent revivals. Shylock has been
played by Charles Calvert, by Forbes-Robertson, by

Beerbohm Tree, F. R. Benson, Arthur Bourchier, Oscar Asche, Norman Forbes, Frank Cellier, and many others. Miss Ellen Terry played Portia again in a revival of the play by Matheson Lang in December, 1904; and Miss Fay Davis and Miss Violet Vanbrugh have also been seen in the part. *The Merchant of Venice* has been acted in Paris by an English company before the war, and during the war behind the lines in France and Belgium. It has been one of the most popular of Shakespeare's plays in Germany, where Schröder and Ludwig Devrient were among the famous actors of Shylock. In America it was first performed by the Hallams at Williamsburg, Virginia, in September, 1752, and was frequently acted by Edwin Booth.

[1926]   HAROLD CHILD.

GLOSSARY

Revised (1962)

Note. Where a pun or quibble is intended, the meanings are distinguished as (*a*) and (*b*).

ABODE, delay; 2. 6. 21

ADDRESS, prepare (cf. *Wint.* 4. 4. 53 'Address yourself to entertain them sprightly'); 2. 9. 19

ADVICE, 'upon more advice,' i.e. upon further consideration; 4. 2. 6

ADVISE, consider, reflect; 1. 1. 142; 2. 1. 42

AFFECTION, disposition, inclination (of the mind or body); 1. 1. 16; 3. 1. 55; 4. 1. 50

AGAIN, in consequence. 'Used to indicate intensity of action' (Onions; cf. O.E.D. 'again' adv. 2); 3. 2. 204

ANGEL, 'an old English gold coin ...having as its device the archangel Michael standing upon and piercing the dragon' (O.E.D.), value about 10*s.*; 2. 7. 56

APPROPRIATION, special attribute; 1. 2. 39

APPROVE, make good, justify; 3. 2. 79

ARGOSY, 'a merchant-vessel of the largest size and burden; esp. those of Ragusa and Venice' (O.E.D.). The word is a corruption of 'Aragouse,' the 16th cent. form of 'Ragusa' (cf. *Sh. Eng.* i. 153); 1. 1. 9

ASPECT, appearance; 1. 1. 54; 2. 1. 8

ASSUME, 'to take to oneself formally the insignia of office or symbol of a vocation' (O.E.D.); 2. 9. 51

ATTENTIVE, observant; 5. 1. 71

BATE, depress, reduce in weight; 3. 3. 32

BLACK-MONDAY, i.e. Easter Monday, the 'movable' day, as Lancelot implies; 2. 5. 25

BLUNT, (*a*) unceremonious, (*b*) not to be sharpened (in reference to lead); 2. 7. 8

BREAK, i.e. break faith, break his day; 1. 3. 133

BREAK UP, to open a letter (i.e. break the wax); 2. 4. 11

CARRION, (i) putrefying; 4. 1. 41; (ii) like a skeleton from which the flesh has rotted away; 2. 7. 63; 3. 1. 33

CATER-COUSIN, 'scarce cater-cousins,' i.e. hardly on speaking terms. The derivation of 'cater' is obscure; O.E.D. is inclined to interpret the phrase as 'originally those who were "cousins" by being catered for or boarded together,' a meaning which would be very apt in the present instance. In Eliz. English, of course, 'cousin' often meant little more than 'acquaintance'; 2. 2. 129

CERECLOTH, winding-sheet (lit. a cloth dipped in melted wax); 2. 7. 51

CHEER, face, countenance (the orig. meaning); 2. 3. 313

CHOIR *vb.*, make music; 5. 1. 63

CHOOSE! do as you please! take your own way! (in mod. slang 'lump it'); v. O.E.D. 4*b*; 1. 2. 45

CIRCUMSTANCE, circumlocution

(cf. *Two Gent.* 1. 1. 36, 37); 1. 1. 154

COLD, 'without power to move or influence' (O.E.D. doubtfully); cf. *Two Gent.* 4. 4. 179 'I hope my master's suit will be but cold'; 2. 7. 73

COLT, 'a young or inexperienced person' (O.E.D.); 1. 2. 38

COMING-IN, 'a simple coming-in,' i.e. a poor allowance (prob. with an indelicate secondary meaning; cf. *Gen.* xix. 31); 2. 2. 161

COMMODITY, (i) goods; 1. 1. 178; (ii) advantage, privileges; 3. 3. 27

COMPLEXION, disposition, nature; 3. 1. 28

COMPROMISED (to be), come to terms, settle differences; 1. 3. 75

CONCEIT, conception, understanding; 3. 4. 2.

CONDITION, disposition, character; 1. 2. 124

CONDITIONED, 'best conditioned' = best tempered, 3. 2. 294

CONSTANT, resolute, self-possessed; 3. 2. 248

CONTAIN, retain, keep in one's possession or under one's control; 4. 1. 50; 5. 1. 202

CONTINENT, 'that which comprises or sums up, the sum and substance' (O.E.D.); 3. 2. 130

COPE. There are two distinct verbs, 'cope,' meaning (i) strike, encounter, have to do with; and (ii) buy, barter, give in exchange for. Shakespeare is not exactly quibbling here, but he seems to have both meanings in mind; 4. 1. 408

COVER, (a) lay the cloth, (b) cover the head; 3. 5. 47, 49

CRISPED, closely and stiffly curled; 3. 2. 92

CURTSY, (a) polite bow (not, as now, confined to feminine genuflexion), (b) a small quantity, a trifle (cf. mod. idiom 'a nodding acquaintance with'); 3. 2. 46

DANGER, 'within his danger,' i.e. in his power, at his mercy (see C. S. Lewis, *Allegory of Love*, p. 364); 4. 1. 177

DEATH, skull; 2. 7. 63

DIMENSIONS, bodily parts; 3. 1. 5

DISABLE, disparage (cf. *A.Y.L.* 4. 1. 32 'disable all the benefit of your own country'); 2. 7. 3

DISCHARGE, pay (a debt), cf. *Errors*, 4. 1. 13 'I will discharge my bond'; 4. 1. 205

DISCOVER, to reveal by drawing aside a curtain. A technical term of the theatre (cf. Chambers, *Eliz. Stage*, iii. 81–2); 2. 7. 1

DISCRETION, discrimination; 3. 60

DISH OF DOVES, i.e. enough doves to fill a dish when cooked; 2. 2. 134

DOIT, 'a small Dutch coin formerly in use...the half of an English farthing...a very small or trifling sum' (O.E.D.); 1. 137

DUCAT, a Spanish gold coin valued under Philip and Mary at 6s. 8d., the 'double ducat' being worth 13s. 4d. (v. *Sh.Eng.* i. 342); 1. 3. 1, etc.

DULL, blunt; 1. 1. 118

DUMB-SHOW, a silent performance of part of a play, intended either to explain briefly the events that pass between two acts, or to foreshadow in emblematic fashion what is to follow; 1. 2. 69

EANLING, new-born lamb; 1. 3. 2

EGALL, equal (the form also occurs in *Titus*, 4. 4. 4, and *R. III*, 3. 7. 213); 3. 4. 13

ECHE, add to, lengthen, increase; 3. 2. 23

ELECTION, making a choice; 2. 9. 3; 3. 2. 24

EREBUS, the classical hell; 5. 1. 88

EVEN, impartial; 2. 7. 25

EXCREMENT, any outgrowth of the body, e.g. hair, nails; 3. 2. 87

FANCY, inclination, baseless supposition, fantasy (of which word it was orig. a contraction); 3. 2. 63, 68, 70

FAVOUR, leniency; 4. 1. 382

FEAR, (i) doubt; 3. 2. 29; (ii) fear for; 3. 5. 3

FIA, mispronunciation of 'via' (q.v.); 2. 2. 10

FILL-HORSE, cart-horse, The 'fills' or 'thrills' were the shafts of a cart; 2. 2. 92

FIND FORTH, find out (cf. *Err.* 1. 2. 37); 1. 1. 143

FLEDGE, an obs. form of 'fledged'; 3. 1. 28

FLIGHT, 'of the self-same flight' = of the same carrying power. A flight really consisted of 'two or three arrows, matched and found to fly exactly alike' (*Sh. Eng.* ii. 381); 1. 1. 141

FOND, foolish; 3. 3. 9

FULSOME, rank; 1. 3. 83

GABERDINE, a long coat, worn loose or girdled with long sleeves—not worn by Jews only (v. Linthicum, pp. 200–01); 1. 3. 109

GAGED, pledged; 1. 1. 130

GAPING PIG, a pig's-head, with its mouth open, prepared for the table. Malone quotes Nashe, *Pierce Penilesse*, 1592, 'Some will take on like a madman if they see a pigge come to the table' (v. McKerrow, *Nashe*, i. 188), and observes that this passage 'perhaps furnished our author with his instance'; 4. 1. 47, 54

GARNISH, outfit, garment; 2. 6. 45

GARNISHED, furnished. Most edd. interpret 'furnished with words'; but surely the meaning is 'with the fool's outfit of motley, cap and bauble'; 3. 5. 64

GEAR, purpose, business; 1. 1. 110; 2. 2. 165

GLEAN, (*a*) glean corn, (*b*) cut off stragglers in battle (cf. 'low peasantry'), O.E.D. 'glean' 3*d*; 2. 9. 46

GOOD, well-to-do; 1. 3. 12

GOODLY, gracious, benign; 3. 5. 45

GRAVEL-BLIND, a jocular link between 'Sand-blind' (q.v.) and Stone-blind; 2. 2. 33

GROW TO, 'a household phrase applied to milk when burnt to the bottom of the saucepan and thence acquiring an unpleasant taste' (Clark and Wright); 2. 2. 16

GUARDED, ornamented with trimming or lace; 2. 2. 154

GUILÉD, treacherous, endowed with guiles (cf. 'delighted,' *Meas.* 3. 1. 120); 3. 2. 97

HEARSED, coffined; 3. 1. 82

HEAVENS (for the), in heaven's name; 2. 2. 11

HIGH-DAY, holiday; 2. 9. 98

HIP (to have upon), a wrestling metaphor (cf. *Sh. Hand*, pp. 165–66); 1. 3. 43; 4. 1. 330

HOVEL-POST, a post used in the making of a stack of corn (v. O.E.D. 'hovel' 4); 2. 2. 64

HUMILITY, humanity (cf. *L.L.L.* 4. 3. 346 'plant in tyrants mild humility'; *Hen. V*, 3. 1. 4; *R. III*, 2. 1. 72); O.E.D. does not notice this meaning; 3. 1. 64

HUSBANDRY, administration of the household; 3. 4. 25

HYRCANIA, the land south of the Caspian Sea, proverbial for wildness and savagery; 2. 7. 41

IMPEACH, discredit, call in question; 3. 2. 279; 3. 3. 29

IMPOSITION, command, charge laid upon one; 1. 2. 99; 3. 4. 33

IMPUGN, dispute the validity of a statement or line of action; 4. 1. 176

INCISION (make), let blood. A technical expression in surgery. (Cf. *L.L.L.* 4. 3. 94 and Jonson, *Cynthia's Revels*, 4. 1., which speaks of a lover 'stabbing himself, drinking healths, or writing languishing letters in his blood'); 2. 1. 6

INFECTION, blunder for 'affection'; 2. 2. 123

INSCULPED, engraved; 2. 7 57.

INTER'GATORY. A reference to Chancery jurisdiction of the period, which 'got at the truth by putting searching interrogations to the defendant himself which he had to answer on oath, and by clapping him in prison if he disobeyed the Chancellor's orders' (*Sh.Eng.* i. 395); 5. 1. 299, 301

INTERMISSION, rest during work; 3. 2. 200

JACK, knave; 3. 4. 77

JEW'S EYE, a proverbial expression for something valued highly (cf. G. Harvey, 1592, 'A soueraine Rule, as deare as a Iewes eye'); 2. 5. 42

JUMP WITH, agree with; 2. 9. 33

KNAP, to bite with a crackling sound; 3. 1. 9

LEAVE, part with, lose (O.E.D. 8 *b*); 5. 1. 151, 173, 197

LEVEL AT, aim at, guess at (lit. to aim with a bow or gun); 1. 2. 36

LICHAS, the servant of Hercules who unwittingly brought his master the Nessus shirt; 2. 1. 32

LIEU, 'in lieu of,' i.e. as a payment for, as a reward for, in acknowledgement of; 4. 1. 406; 5. 1. 263

LIGHT, wanton; 2. 6. 42; 5. 1. 130

LIKELY, comely; 2. 9. 92

LIVERY, the badge of cognizance worn by the retainers of some great lord (cf. *shadowed*); 2. 1. 2

MAGNIFICO, Venetian grandee 3. 2. 281; 4. 1. S.D. head

MANTLE, 'of liquids: to become covered with a coating or scum (O.E.D.) 1. 1. 89

MARK, 'God bless the mark!' O.E.D. explains as 'an exclamatory phrase, prob. originally serving as a formula to avert an evil omen and hence used by way of apology when something horrible, disgusting, indecent or profane has been mentioned (cf. *Two Gent.* 4. 4. 18); 2. 2. 22

MATCH *sb.*, bargain; 3. 1. 41

MERE, sheer, complete; 3. 2. 26

MIND OF LOVE, i.e. love-schemes 'mind' = purpose; 2. 8. 42

MOE, more in number. Formerly 'more' meant 'more in quantity' only; 4. 1. 81

MOIETY, share, portion (lit. half) 4. 1. 26

MORTAL-BREATHING, i.e. like mortal, breathing (and yet saint); 2. 7. 40

MORTIFYING, death-causing. Sighs and groans were supposed to drain the blood (cf. *M.D.N.* 3. 2. 97 note); 1. 1. 82

GLOSSARY

MOTION, inward prompting or impulse, desire, inclination, emotion; 5. 1. 87

MUTUAL, common to more than two. Much more frequently used by Shakespeare in this than in what is now regarded as the only correct sense; 5. 1. 78

NAUGHTY, wicked, good for naught; 3. 3. 9; 5. 1. 92

NEAT'S TONGUE, i.e. a cured or dried ox-tongue; 1. 1. 112

OBLIGED FAITH, 'faith bound by contract' (Aldis Wright); 2. 6. 7

OCCASION, i.e. events as they fall out; 3. 5. 51

OFFENCE, displeasure, annoyance (v. O.E.D. 5*b*); 4. 1. 68

OFFICER, a sheriff's officer, catchpole(cf. *Err.* G. 'sergeant of the band'); 3. 1. 118

OLD. Colloquial, meaning 'plentiful, great'; 4. 2. 15

OPINION, reputation; 1. 1. 91, 102

OSTENT, show, display; 2. 2. 193; 2. 8. 44

O'ER-LOOK. A technical term in witchcraft, meaning 'look upon one with the evil eye' (cf. 'beshrew your eyes'); 3. 2. 15

OVERPEER, tower above; 1. 1. 12

OVER-WEATHERED, worn by exposure to the weather (O.E.D. quotes no other instance); 2. 6. 18

PAGEANT, a movable scaffold on which open-air scenes were enacted or tableaux displayed in the miracle play and civic show (a very apt simile for the Elizabethan argosy); 1. 1. 11

PARCEL, lot, set (contemptuous); 1. 2. 103

PART, depart; 2. 7. 77

PASSION, bodily disorder; 4. 1. 51

PATEN, the small flat dish used with the chalice in the administration of Holy Communion; 5. 1. 60

PAWN, stake, wager; 3. 5. 77

PEEVISH, morose. 'In early quotations often referred to as the result of religious austerities, fasting and the like' (O.E.D.); 1. 1. 86

PEISE THE TIME, (i) 'weigh with deliberation each precious moment' (Clark and Wright), (ii) 'weight the time that it may pass slowly' (Steevens). Whichever interpretation we adopt Shakespeare used the word 'peise' because of its technical associations with the clock, 'peise' being the regular name for the weights used in winding; 3. 2. 22

PENT-HOUSE, v. note; 2. 6. 1

PICK, select, pick out carefully; 2. 9. 48

PILL, peel, strip (v. note); 1. 3. 81

PIRE, peer, examine closely. The form 'peer' is not found before 1590; cf. note; 1. 1. 19

PORT, grand or expensive style of living; 1. 1. 124

POSSESSED, informed; 1. 3. 61

POST, courier, messenger; 2. 9. 100

POSY, 'a short motto, originally a line of verse of poetry and usually in patterned language, inscribed on a knife, within a ring, as a heraldic motto, etc.' (O.E.D.); 5. 1. 149, 152

PRESENTLY, immediately; 1. 1. 183

PREST, ready; 1. 1. 160

PREVENT, forestall, anticipate; 1. 1. 61

PRIZE, match contest; 3. 2. 141

PURCHASE, acquire, gain; 2. 9. 43

QUAINT, skilful, cunning, knowing; 2. 4. 6; 3. 4. 69

QUALIFY, moderate, temper; 4. 1. 7

QUALITY, (i) manner, style; 3. 2. 6; (ii) trait, human characteristic ('the quality of mercy' = the quality, mercy); 4. 1. 181

RACE, herd, stud; 5. 1. 73

RACK, stretch; 1. 1. 181

RATE, *sb.* style, mode of living; 1. 1. 127

RATE, *vb.* value; 2. 7. 26

REASON, talk, hold conversation with; 2. 8. 27

REBEL, *vb.*, lust (cf. *All's. Q.*); 3. 1. 33

REED-VOICE, a reedy or squeaking voice (apparently a technical term in music, v. *Sh.Eng.* ii. 45); 3. 4. 67

REGREETS, salutations; 2. 9. 89

REHEARSE, mention, formally recite; 4. 1. 358

RESPECT (without), without reference to other things (cf. *Ham.* 2. 2. 255 'There is nothing either good or bad, but thinking makes it so'); 5. 1. 100

RESPECTIVE, careful, regardful; 5. 1. 157

REST, 'set up one's rest,' i.e. to be determined, resolved. The expression, derived from the card-game, primero, in which 'the rest' was the name for the reserved stakes, originaly meant 'to hazard one's all'; 2. 2. 100

RHENISH, a white wine from the Rhine, such as hock or moselle; 1. 2. 91; 3. 1. 38

RIALTO, the Exchange in Venice (completed 1591); 1. 3. 19, etc.

RIB, enclose; 2. 7. 51

ROAD, roadstead; 1. 1. 19

ROTH, obs. spelling of 'ruth' = calamity, grief; 2. 9. 78

RUIN, rubbish, refuse; 2. 9. 48

SAD, sober, serious; 2. 2. 193

SAND-BLIND, partially blind, probably a perversion of the O.E. 'samblind' = half-blind (O.E.D.); 2. 2. 33, 71

SCANT, limit, restrict, cut short; 2. 1. 17; 5. 1. 142

SCAPE, escapade; 2. 2. 164

SCARFÉD, decked with streamers; 2. 6. 15

SCRUBBED, undersized, insignifi-

SEASON, alleviate, temper (lit. to mix something with food to make it more palatable; 3. 2. 76; 4. 1. 194

SENSE (in all), on every account; 5. 1. 137

SENSIBLE, substantial, tangible; 2. 9. 89

SENTENCES, maxims; 1. 2. 9

SERVITOR, attendant (a theatrical term); 2. 9. S.D. head

SET FORTH, (a) extol, (b) serve up at table; 3. 5. 85

SET UP ONE'S REST, v. *rest*; 2. 2. 100

SHADOWED, shaded, umbrated (a heraldic term); 2. 1. 2.

SHRINE, i.e. image of a saint or god. This sense not found outside Shakespeare (but cf. *Lucr* 194, *Cymb.* 5. 5. 164); 2. 7. 40

SIBYLLA, the Sibyl of Cumae, keeper of the Sibylline books, to whom Apollo granted that her years should be as many as the grains in a handful of sand; 1. 2. 101

SIMPLE, poor, wretched, pitiful; 2. 2. 159, 161

SIMPLICITY, folly; 1. 3. 40

SINGLE BOND. Meaning doubtful; either (i) unconditional bond, or (ii) a bond without the name

GLOSSARY

of the sureties attached; 1. 3. 142

SLIPS OF PROLIXITY, lapses into tediousness; 3. 1. 11

SLUBBER, perform in a slovenly manner (lit. daub); 2. 8. 39

SMACK, savour of, be strongly suggestive of; 2. 2. 16

SMUG, trim, neat; 2. 1. 43

SONTIES, saints—diminutive of 'sont,' an old form of 'saint'; 2. 2. 41

SOON AT, towards, near (of time); 2. 3. 5

SOPHY, formerly a title of the Shah of Persia (1500–1736); 2. 1. 25

SORT, *sb.* manner, method; 1. 2. 99

SORT, *vb.* ordain, dispose (cf. *R. III*, 2. 3. 36 'if God sort it so'); 5. 1. 133

SPIRITS, 'faculties of perception' (O.E.D. 18); 5. 1. 71

SUFFICIENT, substantial, well-to-do, financially sound; 1. 3. 17, 25

SULTAN SOLYMAN, Solyman the Magnificent, Sultan of Turkey 1490–1566, who in 1535 undertook a campaign against the Persians; 2. 1. 26

TABLE. In palmistry the 'table' is the quadrangular space formed by the four principal 'lines' in the palm of the hand; 2. 2. 157

TERMS, 'in terms of,' in respect of; 2. 1. 13

THRIFT, (i) thriving, success; 1. 1. 175; (ii) gain, profit; 1. 3. 47, 87

TIME, time of life, age (here 'youth'); 1. 1. 129

TOUCH, note, strain (lit. the fingering of the instrument); 5. 1. 58

TRANSECT, prob. misprint of

'traject' (It. *traghetto*, ferry); 3. 4. 53

TUCKET, a flourish on a trumpet; 5. 1. 122 S.D.

TURN TO. (Cf. *M.W.W.* 2. 1. 164 'turn her loose to him,' 168 'turn them together' and *Temp.* 2. 1. 124 note); 1. 3. 78; 3. 4. 78

TYRANNY, cruelty; 4. 1. 13

UNBATED, unabated; 2. 6. 11

UNFURNISHED, unprovided with its fellow; 3. 2. 126

UNHANDLED, not broken in; 5. 1. 73

UNTREAD, retrace; 2. 6. 10

VAIL, lower; 1. 1. 28

VANTAGE, opportunity (Portia is thinking of some game or contest); 3. 2. 175

VENDIBLE, 'a maid not vendible,' i.e. an old maid past marriageable age (lit. past her market); 1. 1. 112

VENTURE, commercial speculation (cf. *Sh.Eng.* i. 334); 1. 1. 15, 21, 42; 1. 3. 20

VIA, 'an adverb of encouraging much used by commanders, as also by riders to their horses' (Florio). Lancelot pronounces the word 'Fia'; 2. 2. 10

WARRANTY, authorisation; 1. 1. 132

WELL TO LIVE, in capital health (cf. 'well-to-do'); 2. 2. 49

WIND ABOUT. A metaphor from stalking game: we should say 'beat about the bush'; 1. 1. 154

WORD, pithy sentence; 4. 1. 337

YOUNGER, the younger son of the parable (cf. *Luke* xv. 12). Rowe read 'younker' (cf. 3 *Hen. VI*,

2. 1. 24 'trimmed like a younker prancing to his love'); the meaning is the same, and it is clear from 1 *Hen. IV*, 3. 3. 92 that 'younker' was simply another name for the Prodigal Son; 2. 6. 14

YOUNG-EYED, i.e. with sight ever young. Mediaeval tradition endowed the Cherubim with a peculiar power of seeing, and in the three other places where Shakespeare mentions them the notion of keen sight is introduced (cf. *Ham.* 4. 3. 50; *Macb.* 1. 7. 22–4; *Troil.* 3. 2. 74–5). We are indebted to Verity for this note; 5. 1. 63